Humanising IT™

The Experience Distortion of IT Service Management

Katrina Macdermid
Co-Founder & Designer: HIT Global Limited

When the first edition of Human-Centred Design for IT Service Management was published in 2022, I hoped it would spark a conversation. What I didn't expect was how global that conversation would become.

Copyright © 2026 HIT Global Limited

All rights reserved.

No part of this publication may be reproduced, stored, or transmitted in any form or by any means, electronic, mechanical, photocopying, recording, scanning, or otherwise, without written permission from the publisher.

ISBN: 978-1-0684675-2-3

Table of contents

Foreword 4

Prelude 6

Is IT Responsible for Experience? 6

Changing the ITSM Agenda 9

What This Book Is 12

Who This Book Is For 13

Scope of This Book 14

How to Use This Book 15

Chapter 1: The Experience We Didn't Design 17

Chapter 2: What Traditional ITSM Was Never Designed to Address 21

Chapter 3: Parallel Disciplines, Divergent Purposes 31

Chapter 4: Introducing the HIT DDF™ 36

Chapter 5: Diamond One – Phase 1 49

Chapter 6: Diamond One – Phase 2 110

Chapter 6: Diamond Two – Phase 3 143

Chapter 7: Diamond Two – Phase 4 156

Chapter 8: Maintain & Run 166

Applying the HIT Double Diamond Framework™ in Practice 172

Closing Reflection 180

Foreword

Katrina's first book, *Human-Centred Design for IT Service Management*, was groundbreaking. It challenged service management's collective wisdom by introducing experience and human-centred design into a discipline long dominated by process, compliance, and control. At a time when IT success was measured largely through tickets, tools, and frameworks, Katrina asked a far more provocative question: *how does IT actually feel to the people it serves?*

The second edition of *Human-Centred Design for IT Service Management* remains the top-selling book at industry events and continues to be in high demand through the HIT Global website. Its enduring success reflects not only the strength of the ideas, but how deeply they resonated with practitioners who instinctively knew something vital was missing from traditional approaches to IT service management.

So why this new book?

Because over the past three years, *Humanising IT*™ has evolved from an idea into a movement. What began as a challenge to conventional thinking has become a transformative leadership philosophy and a globally adopted training programme, embraced by individuals and organisations across sectors, geographies, and levels of seniority. In that time, Katrina's thinking — and the conversations she has helped shape — have matured significantly.

Humanising IT™ is not an update or a reworking of earlier material. It goes further, addressing a more urgent challenge: how leaders design and govern IT services in a world shaped by accelerating change, rising expectations, and the growing influence of AI. As technology becomes more powerful and pervasive, experience, trust, and outcomes matter more than ever.

The book recognises a critical truth: good experiences are not the result of heroic individuals compensating for broken systems, nor of impressive technology poorly integrated into real working lives. They are the product of intentional design, aligning technology, behaviour, culture, and decision-making so that systems work *with* people, not against them.

At its core, this book is about a mindset shift — from process compliance to meaningful impact; from efficiency metrics to lived experience; from doing IT *to* people, to designing services *with* them. In an AI-enabled world, this shift is essential, as poorly designed services can scale frustration just as easily as efficiency.

Crucially, this book offers practical guidance on how to implement and embed Humanising IT™ into an organisation's culture and ways of working — shaping behaviours, leadership decisions, and service design so that human experience becomes the default, not an afterthought.

I have had the privilege of working alongside Katrina as this thinking has evolved in classrooms, boardrooms, and real organisations, and I have seen first-hand the impact that human-centred, experience-led approaches can have when applied with intent and integrity.

If IT is to remain relevant, trusted, and valued in the age of AI, it must become more human. This book shows why and importantly how that journey begins.

Mark Basham,

Mark Basham, Co-Founder & CEO, HIT Global Limited

Prelude

Is IT Responsible for Experience?

It is a question I am often asked, by IT professionals and by those outside the function — and it is one of the reasons this book exists.

It is also why I chose its title.

Because there *is* a **distortion** in how experience is currently understood within our industry.

Experience has become the new must-have in IT service management. It is discussed widely, measured inconsistently, and too often treated as something to be "managed" in the same way we manage processes, tools, or data.

That framing concerns me.

In my view, IT service management is not responsible for experience in its entirety.
Humanising IT™ is explicit on this point.

IT does not own experience.
It does not control experience.

Experience is shaped by many factors outside IT's remit — organisational culture, leadership behaviour, physical environments, policies, incentives, and constraints that no system can resolve. IT cannot be accountable for all of that, nor should it try to be.

And yet, somewhere along the way, experience has become distorted within IT service management.

This distortion is compounded by a second misunderstanding.

Experience frameworks such as human-centred design, on which Humanising IT™ is based, were never created for the operational, regulatory, and risk-laden environment of IT service management. They were designed for exploration, discovery, and innovation — not for environments governed by security controls, compliance obligations, service continuity, and accountability at scale.

Treating these approaches as if they can be applied to IT service management unchanged is one of the industry's quiet misconceptions. Assuming that adopting the language of experience automatically resolves this mismatch only deepens the distortion.

Not because IT does not care —
but because IT has increasingly been asked to take responsibility for something it was never designed to own, using tools and structures built for governance, control, and operational stability, not lived human experience.

What I will concede, and what this book is built on, is this:

As technology has become embedded in almost every task, system, and interaction, IT now plays a significant and increasingly visible role in shaping how work is experienced.

When systems are slow, rigid, opaque, or poorly aligned to real work, people feel it.
When services are clear, supportive, and well-designed, people feel that too.

This matters.

If IT attempts to manage experience as a whole, it risks overreach. If IT ignores experience entirely, it risks designing services that perform well operationally while creating friction, workarounds, and unintended consequences in real environments.

This tension, between responsibility and ownership, intention and lived reality, is what I refer to as **the experience distortion of IT service management**.

Humanising IT™ sits between these extremes.

It recognises that IT is not the sole owner of experience, but that it does have a critical responsibility: to understand how its services are experienced, and to design and operate them with that reality in mind.

I hope you enjoy my book.

Changing the ITSM Agenda

When my first book *Human-Centred Design for IT Service Management* was published in 2022, I hoped it would spark a conversation. What I didn't expect was how global that conversation would become.

In the years that followed, that work evolved into the HIT Double Diamond (HIT DDF™) a framework that brings human-centred design into the full lifecycle of IT services, including IT Operations and the foundation on which this new book is built.

Since then, Humanising IT™ and the HIT DDF™ have been adopted across industries and continents. Today, teams in organisations of every size are using its experience-led principles to rethink how IT services are understood, designed, delivered and supported.

At the same time, the nature of IT work is changing.

AI is accelerating service delivery, compressing decision cycles, and automating work that once absorbed significant human effort. But it is also making something increasingly visible: Many of the assumptions embedded in our services, processes, and tools no longer hold.

This is not a threat to the profession.
It is an opportunity for expansion.

IT professionals already hold deep expertise in systems, services, and operational reliability. Humanising IT™ extends that expertise into experience, providing the skills, language, and structure needed to design services that work not only in theory, but in lived reality.

This book reflects what has been learned through years of application: across workshops, organisations, industries, and real operating environments. It captures the patterns that repeat, the tensions that persist, and the conditions under which IT services succeed or fail from a human perspective.

Future publications, including *Humanising AI*™, will explore the intersection of experience and intelligent systems in greater depth. This book focuses on the foundation: understanding experience as an operational concern, not an abstract ideal.

And on that note…

My catchphrase used to be *"making ITSM human-centred."*
But I've evolved and so has the work.

Now, it's about **changing the agenda for ITSM and the wonderful humans who work within it.**

Katrina Macdermid
Co-Founder & Designer: HIT Global Limited

What This Book Is

This book is a practical guide to applying human-centred design within ITSM. Inside, you'll find:

- Practical tools
- Human-centred techniques
- Methods refined through years of real-world application
- Patterns and insights drawn from global practice

…all designed for real-world use.

This book works alongside established ITSM frameworks, strengthening them with a practical human-centred layer that supports better decisions, clearer understanding, and more meaningful experiences.

Whether you are designing a new service, improving a process, or rethinking your operating model, it offers the mindset and methods to make experience an intentional part of how IT works.

It's built on one core principle:

Every IT process is a human touchpoint, shaping the experience of both the people who use IT services and the people who support them.

Who This Book Is For

This book is for anyone who:
- Designs, delivers, or supports IT services
- Wants to strengthen relationships with users and stakeholders
- Wants simpler, more human-focused ways of working
- Wants to understand how people experience IT
- Wants practical, immediately applicable tools — not theory

From service desk analysts to CIOs, and every role in between. If you work with IT services, this book is for you.

Scope of This Book

This book introduces the HIT DDF™ in its entirety, while focusing in depth on **Phase 1: Discover/Strategy** and **Phase 2: Define/Plan**—the stages where assumptions are surfaced, behaviours are examined, and the true nature of the problem is established.

This emphasis is deliberate. These early phases are where ITSM most often struggles, and where Humanising IT™ creates the greatest shift in thinking, practice, and organisational understanding.

The later phases —**Develop/Design, Deliver/Build/Transition, and Maintain / Run** are outlined at a conceptual level in this volume with selected activities explored. Their detailed methods and tools will be explored in future publications with the same depth and rigour applied here.

How to Use This Book

Use this book as both a practical guide and a reference.

It will walk you through the full HIT DDF™, while providing step-by-step depth on the early activities that shape every decision that follows. These chapters are designed to be applied immediately in your own environment.

As outlined, the later phases of the framework are introduced conceptually here, with deeper, hands-on application delivered through facilitated HIT Masterclasses in both online and in-person formats.

What Comes Next

This book acknowledges the achievements of ITSM.

ITSM has enabled organisations to operate, scale, trade, employ people, and deliver services reliably. These outcomes are not accidental, they are the result of sustained investment, discipline, and professional practice.

The chapters that follow explore:

- Why good processes fail in real environments
- Why users behave differently from what we expect
- Why IT and the business talk past each other
- Why friction persists even in well-run organisations
- Why experience is the missing dimension in most IT decisions

Only then will we introduce the HIT Double Diamond (HIT DDF™) — the framework developed by HIT Global Limited that integrates human-centred design into ITSM.

Before we begin Chapter 1, I invite you to pause and reflect on the everyday experiences that shape how IT is understood. The following section provides the context for why this work matters and why I wrote this book.

Chapter 1

The Experience We Didn't Design

In IT, it's reasonable to believe we understand our users.

We talk to them.
We support them.
We monitor their systems.
We analyse their incidents.
We close their tickets.

But our research reveals a different story.

When IT professionals were asked what they believe the business thinks of IT, the dominant words were:

Slow.
Complicated.
Confusing.
Disjointed.
Hard work.
Essential… but frustrating.

And the most confronting part?

They came from IT professionals who care deeply, who are trying to do the right thing, and who are often working within systems that were never designed to make the work feel simple.

These words were not offered defensively or dismissively.
They reflect care and professionalism — not a lack of skill or intent, but an experience that has largely **grown organically over time**, rather than being intentionally shaped.

These experiences often carry the loudest voice in how IT is perceived — even as they sit alongside decades of remarkable ITSM work. At the same time, ITSM has increasingly been asked to take responsibility for experience — something it was never originally designed to do.

And experience cannot be created through instruction alone. You cannot simply tell a team to be "more user-focused," in the same way you cannot tell someone to be happier, taller, or more confident.

Good intent is not enough.

Designing for experience requires foundational understanding, shared language, practical techniques, and space to observe how work actually happens — before solutions are imposed.

Just as IT professionals build capability through training and education, experience-led work also requires structured learning.

After all, we wouldn't ask a software engineer to write a human resources policy without training, nor ask a Chief Financial Officer to run a change advisory board.

Unless they are understood and addressed, these experiences are likely to be scaled by AI, shaping perception in ways that can overshadow the foundations that made AI possible in the first place.

The Human System AI Will Inherit

It would be remiss and arguably incomplete to publish anything on modern ITSM without addressing the role of artificial intelligence. We are living through the fastest technological acceleration in human history.

AI is reshaping how organisations operate, how decisions are made, how information flows, and how work gets done.

Boards are demanding more AI.
CIOs are under pressure to "use AI more."
Teams are being asked to automate faster, scale faster, decide faster.

But beneath this global push sits something that must be acknowledged:

AI does not generate new logic independently. It derives its reasoning from the patterns, structures, and assumptions embedded in the data and environments it is trained on.

And in many organisations, the logic that underpins ITSM is being asked to do far more than it was ever designed for.

This is where Humanising IT™ becomes essential.

AI will inherit the systems, processes, behaviours, and experiences we have today — not the ones we wish we had. If those systems are fragmented, complex, or misaligned with how people actually work, AI will scale those patterns just as efficiently as it scales the good ones.

Humanising IT™ brings the human context, behavioural insight, and practical design techniques needed to ensure that the systems AI learns from and ultimately amplifies reflect the realities of modern work and the people who do it.

What Is Humanising IT™?

And of course, before we proceed, we need to define what Humanising IT™ is.

Humanising IT™ is the integration of applicable human-centred design tools and techniques into the ITSM lifecycle. It recognises the constraints, responsibilities, and operational realities of ITSM, and adapts experience-led methods so they work within those boundaries.

It is not design thinking applied to IT.
It is design translated for IT.

Humanising IT™ provides the practical mindset, methods, and behavioural insight needed to design services that work for people and systems while respecting the governance, scale, and accountability that IT carries.

This is the foundation for the HIT DDF™.

Chapter 2

What Traditional ITSM Was Never Designed to Address

We exposed the urgency created by AI the risk that automation can magnify certain blind spots while overshadowing the successes of ITSM, this chapter looks further back. It asks a harder question:

How did the gap between IT and human experience form in the first place?

The answer lies in original design intent.

ITSM was created to manage technology to bring stability, control, and reliability to increasingly complex systems. It was not designed to understand human behaviour, context, or lived experience.

As technology has expanded into every role, every process, and every moment of work, that original focus is now being asked to stretch further than it was ever intended, becoming one of the central challenges facing modern IT organisations.

The Industrial DNA Inside ITSM

When ITSM emerged in the 1980s and 1990s, it borrowed heavily from the dominant logic of the time: industrial engineering and manufacturing. Henry Ford's gospel of standardisation was everywhere — in production lines, logistics, and eventually in technology management.

> *ITSM adopted many elements of the industrial mindset — implicitly, not deliberately.*

Uniformity was the goal.
Variation was the enemy.
Process created safety.
Consistency ensured stability.

And for the world IT operated in back then centralised data centres, batch processing, sequential workflows this model was perfect.

The dominant management logic of the time emphasised:

- Standardisation
- Repeatability
- Control
- Error reduction
- Predictability

But today's world is nothing like that.

Before Technology Became the Workplace

When ITSM first emerged, technology was used by a relatively small number of specialists within an organisation, a reality that feels almost unrecognisable today.

Typically, these included:

- Systems operators running mainframes and data centres
- Programmers and application developers
- Database administrators
- Infrastructure and network engineers
- Finance and payroll teams processing batch jobs
- Operations staff supporting back-office systems

What Traditional ITSM Was Never Designed to Address

> *In that context, IT was something that was managed, not something that was experienced.*

Most employees did not interact directly with IT systems at all.

Work was paper-based.
Requests were manual.
Processing happened in batches.
Interfaces were technical.
Access was controlled.

The management logic that shaped early ITSM reflected the broader industrial thinking of the time. Organisations prioritised standardisation, repeatability, and control to reduce risk and ensure stability.

Process created safety. Consistency enabled scale.

The Invisible Work No Dashboard Ever Shows

Every organisation carries two layers of work:

1. The formal work people are hired to do.
2. The quiet, often unseen work they do to make systems, processes, and expectations function in practice.

This second layer is rarely measured, rarely acknowledged, and almost never seen by IT.

Yet it shapes people's experience of technology far more than official incidents ever will.

People:

- Restart frozen apps
- Avoid logging tickets out of frustration
- Ask colleagues instead of IT
- Write their own personal instructions
- Accept failures as "normal"
- Silently work around the system because it feels easier

A dashboard will never show these moments. But they define the organisation's emotional truth about IT.

The absence of a ticket does not mean the absence of a problem. It often means the problem is being handled elsewhere — or not at all.

What Gets Measured Gets Managed

The phrase *"what gets measured gets managed"* is commonly attributed to **Peter Drucker**, and while its precise origin is debated, the principle itself is well established in management practice. Measurement directs attention. Attention shapes decision-making. Over time, what is measured becomes what organisations optimise.

In ITSM, this relationship between measurement and management has been fundamental to building reliable, scalable, and controlled technology environments.

To understand how this plays out, it is useful to clarify two core constructs.

***Service Level Agreements (SLAs)** define expected levels of service between a service provider and its customer. These typically include measures such as response times, resolution targets, availability, or uptime. In many organisations, SLAs also carry commercial implications, such as service credits or financial penalties when commitments are not met. They emerged to support reliability, manage downtime, and clarify expectations in environments where technology stability was — and remains — critical.*

***Operational Level Agreements (OLAs)** are internal agreements within the service provider organisation that define how teams support one another to meet SLA commitments. They are not visible to the business and do not carry financial penalties or rewards. Their role is operational coordination rather than commercial enforcement.*

Both SLAs and OLAs were created with clear and appropriate intentions: standardisation, risk control, and predictability.

They reflect a period in which stabilising technology was the primary concern, and measurement was designed accordingly.

What Traditional ITSM Was Never Designed to Address

While updated frameworks such as ITIL 4 no longer distinguish formally between SLAs and OLAs, the underlying dynamics remain: external commitments shape expectations, and internal agreements shape the ability to meet them.

With these constructs clarified, we can return to the broader question of how measurement shapes what ITSM pays attention to.

"You may be familiar with the term watermelon reporting — dashboards that look green on the surface while the lived experience beneath them is unmistakably red. The example below illustrates how this plays out in practice.

What Traditional ITSM Was Never Designed to Address

Example of Watermelon Reporting

A service provider reports 100% SLA compliance for incident response and resolution.

All OLAs between internal teams are also marked fully met.
On paper, everything is green.

But underneath:

- *Incidents are closed quickly to meet SLA clocks, not because the issue is truly resolved*

- *Teams pass tickets between groups to satisfy OLA handoff times*

- *Root causes remain unaddressed because they fall outside SLA scope*

- *Employees experience recurring disruptions but stop logging tickets because "IT just closes them anyway"*

- *The same issue reappears weekly, but each occurrence is treated as a new, isolated incident*

- *The business experiences instability, frustration, and lost productivity — none of which appear in SLA or OLA metrics*

- *Operationally, the numbers are green.*

Experientially, the service is red.

That's watermelon reporting: **Metrics that signal success while the lived experience tells a different story.**

The example above is not an anomaly; it reflects a broader pattern in how ITSM measures performance. In practice, ITSM continues to emphasise measures such as:

- Tickets rather than trust
- Process rather than purpose
- Availability rather than outcome

These measures are effective at managing operational performance. They enable consistency, comparability, and governance at scale.

However, because measurement shapes management focus, aspects of experience that are not measured tend to receive less attention. This reflects a broader pattern in how performance is represented and understood.

This is not ITSM failing. It is ITSM measuring exactly what it was built to measure.

> *This is not ITSM failing. It is ITSM measuring exactly what it was built to measure.*

The metrics used in ITSM were designed to capture system performance, not the lived, emotional, or environmental experience of work.

Emerging Measurement Models

(A Positive Shift — But Not the Whole Solution)

Different regions and sectors use different labels —outcome-based agreements, experience level agreements, experience metrics. These ideas have existed for some time (my ITIL Master thesis in 2015 explored outcome-based agreements).

What is emerging now is a wider awareness that **metrics alone cannot create a better experience**.
The system underneath — the processes, behaviours, interactions, governance, and decision-making — must evolve too.

Changing the metric without changing the system changes nothing.

You can rename the measure, redesign the dashboard, or introduce a new acronym... but unless the underlying ways of working evolve, the experience will not change.

It's like trying to improve a soccer match by adjusting the scoreboard. You don't transform the game by changing how goals are counted. You transform it by coaching differently, playing differently, thinking differently, behaving differently.

The Most Influential Framework in ITSM

Because this book sits firmly within the world of ITSM, it would be incomplete not to reference the frameworks that have shaped how ITSM is practised today.

There are many ITSM frameworks and models you may be familiar with — IT4IT, USM, COBIT, VeriSM, MOF, and others. Each plays a role in certain industries, regions, or contexts.

But the most widely adopted by far is **ITIL®**.

Whether teams follow it formally, informally, lightly, strictly, or simply inherit its language, most IT departments use ITIL in one way or another. It is the common backbone of modern ITSM thinking.

That is why we focus on it here.

Not because ITIL is the most widely adopted framework,
or the "best,"
or the one this book promotes,
but because:

ITIL has shaped the mental models, terminology, processes, and expectations of the ITSM profession more than any other framework over the past four decades.

Understanding those foundations helps us understand the shift the profession is now navigating.

(You will see later that, just as ITSM has multiple frameworks, human-centred design does as well, but for now, we remain focused on the ITSM side of the story.)

A Brief Look at the People Who Created ITIL

To understand why ITSM sometimes feels out of step with today's world, it helps to look at the context in which it was created. ITIL emerged from a group of highly skilled, technically minded professionals in the UK government during the late 1980s and early 1990s. Their expertise was in:

- Operations
- Infrastructure
- Mainframes and networks
- Risk management
- Service continuity
- Engineering discipline

Human-centred design, behavioural science, and ethnographic methods and skills were largely situated outside the prevailing management and operational frameworks shaping ITSM at the time.

Given the challenges organisations faced then, this expertise was not required for ITSM's original mandate.

The problems of the time were technical, not experiential.

Their mandate was simple: **make technology stable and safe**.
And they succeeded.

When a framework is shaped by a focus on stability and designed for an era defined by predictability, it naturally prioritises control, consistency, and risk management over experiential considerations.

This is not a criticism of ITIL or those involved in its creation.

It reflects a broader principle: frameworks inherit the assumptions and priorities of the contexts in which they emerge.

A Note on ITIL's Evolution

The tension observed today arises because the nature of work, human interaction, and operating environments has evolved significantly, while many foundational mental models within ITSM have remained largely consistent.

ITIL has evolved significantly since its earliest versions. Practices have been modernised, language has shifted, and the framework has adapted to new ways of working.

At the same time, its centre of gravity — its foundational purpose — remains aligned with what it was originally designed to achieve: bringing stability, control, and standardisation to technology services. In this role, ITIL continues to be highly effective.

What ITIL was never designed for, and still does not prioritise, is the lived human experience:

- How people feel when technology breaks
- How environments shape behaviour
- How frontline work differs from office work
- How emotional load influences usability
- How service design must accommodate real human constraints

This is not a flaw it is a limitation of a framework built for a different era, by people solving different problems.

Which is why Humanising IT™ does not replace ITIL.
It complements it by adding the lens it has always lacked:
An understanding of human experience.

Chapter 3

Parallel Disciplines, Divergent Purposes

For years, two worlds have existed side by side in organisations.

ITSM and human-centred design.

Both are disciplined.
Both are structured.
Both aim to improve how people interact with services.

They emerged, however, in different eras, contexts, were shaped by different priorities, and were designed to solve different kinds of problems.

What ITSM Was Created to Do

As discussed in Chapter 2, ITSM was established with a clear and enduring purpose.

Its role is to provide stability, control, and reliability for technology services operating at scale, and in many organisations, it continues to do this effectively and consistently.

Because of this focus, ITSM naturally expressed its value through structure: defined processes, governance models, and lifecycle discipline.

Those outside IT encounter the outcomes of this work differently. Rather than engaging with process constructs, best practice frameworks or maturity models, users encounter services through individual moments, when work is interrupted, when systems are unavailable, when support is needed, and when normal operation is restored.

These different viewpoints reflect distinct vantage points rather than shortcomings. ITSM operates according to its design intent, while the experience of its outputs is interpreted through the lens of day-to-day work.

> *One of the core insights behind Humanising IT™ is that you cannot simply drop human-centred design into ITSM and expect it to work. It's the square-peg-in-a-round-hole problem: the methods were created for different environments, with different constraints, rhythms, and responsibilities.*
>
> *Humanising IT™ takes the intent of human-centred design and reshapes it for a world defined by governance, scale, risk, and accountability — making experience work practical, relevant, and achievable inside IT.*

This distinction is not about right or wrong.
It reflects the fact that ITSM was designed to manage services and technology performance, rather than to analyse or interpret human experience.

What Human-Centred Design Was Created to Do

Human-centred design is a structured, disciplined approach to problem-solving. Like ITSM, it is built on established frameworks, repeatable methods, and a clear sequence of activities. Its discipline lies in understanding people in context before deciding what to change.

> *Human-centred design, contrary to common belief, is not about making things attractive or creating exceptional experiences. It is a disciplined way of understanding what shapes people's actions so systems can be designed to work in the real world.*

It focuses on:

- Observing real behaviour, not reported behaviour
- Understanding environments, constraints, and pressures
- Uncovering unmet needs and hidden assumptions
- Designing solutions that work in practice, not just in theory

Human-centred design is not about asking people what they want. It is about understanding what shapes their actions — and designing accordingly.

This approach has long been recognised in design disciplines: understanding people does not come from asking them what they want, but from observing how they behave within real constraints.

A Simple Example of Human-Centred Design

Consider the experience of a traveller arriving at a modern airport.

When the experience works well, it feels seamless:

- It's immediately clear where to go
- Signage is consistent and visible from a distance
- Check-in options are obvious — staffed counters, self-service kiosks, bag-drop lanes
- The sequence of steps makes sense without explanation
- Printing a boarding pass or tagging a bag is straightforward
- Queues are organised in ways that reduce confusion and stress

None of this is accidental.

Human-centred design looks at the *entire journey*: travellers arriving tired, rushed, carrying luggage, managing children, navigating unfamiliar spaces, dealing with time pressure, or feeling anxious about travel. Designers observe how people behave in these real conditions and shape the system — signage, layout, flow, options, interfaces, and support — around actual behaviour rather than internal process maps.

When aligned, the experience feels effortless.

When misaligned, friction is immediate and memorable.

That is human-centred design.

It complements system design by examining how work is carried out in real conditions.

A Simple Example of ITSM

Since we've shown a simple example of human-centred design, it's useful to balance it with an equally simple example from ITSM — a moment every practitioner recognises, where the work is structured, fast-paced, and lived under real conditions.

Consider a familiar moment inside IT: a Priority 2 incident is raised and the team begins managing it.

When the process works as designed, it looks orderly:

- The incident is assigned to the right team
- The analyst follows the documented steps
- Updates are added at the expected intervals
- Escalation rules are clear
- Communication follows the template
- The workflow moves predictably toward resolution

But in real conditions, the experience is very different:

- The analyst is juggling multiple incidents
- Information arrives incomplete or out of sequence
- Teams work in parallel, not in the neat order the process assumes
- People rely on shortcuts learned through experience
- Updates lag behind the work because the situation moves faster than the system
- The "official" workflow bends to fit what's actually happening

None of this is unusual.

This is everyday ITSM: a system designed to create order in the middle of real-world complexity.

Why the Two Worlds Evolved Separately

When ITIL and other ITSM frameworks were created, technology environments were largely centralised and accessed by specialist users.

Parallel Disciplines, Divergent Purposes

In that context, experience was not a primary consideration, digital systems were predictable, tightly controlled, and often optional.

Meanwhile, disciplines such as human-centred design, user experience, and service design were emerging in industries where experience directly influenced adoption, satisfaction, and success. These fields developed in competitive environments where simplicity, clarity, and emotional response mattered.

Early e-commerce companies quickly learned that confusing navigation or unclear language meant lost sales.

In a market where customers could leave with a single click, experience directly determined success. This environment accelerated the growth of disciplines focused on clarity, ease, and emotional reassurance.

But ITSM evolved without this mindset.

ITSM evolved with a focus on control and reliability. Design disciplines evolved with a focus on connection and understanding.

Both produced extraordinary results within the contexts for which they were designed.

As digital experiences became embedded across every role, workflow, and organisational interaction, it became increasingly evident that these disciplines were addressing different aspects of the same reality.

As my career in ITSM progressed, and my study and application of human-centred design deepened, it became clear:

Each discipline was accomplishing a different dimension of the same challenge.

This book is written to bring those worlds together — and to show what becomes possible when they do.

Chapter 4

Introducing the HIT DDF™

Why a Design Model Was Needed in ITSM

Disciplines evolve when their underlying thinking evolves.
For ITSM, that shift is Humanising IT™, and the HIT DDF™ is the model that enables it.

To understand the origins of the HIT DDF™, we return to where this thinking began. Not inside IT, but inside the British Design Council, which in 2004 introduced a simple model that reshaped the design world: the Double Diamond.

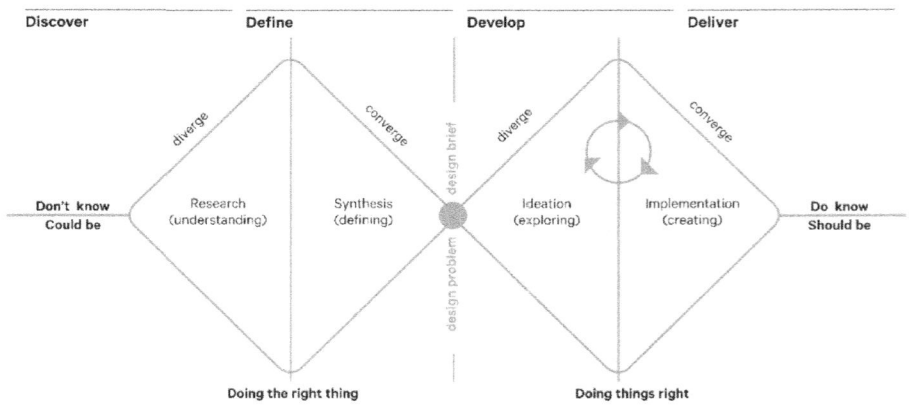

Figure 1: *Double Diamond by the British Design Council*

Introducing the HIT DDF™

Before the model, design work was inconsistent, unstructured, and hard to explain. Designers were doing good work, but:

- Designers used different words
- The process was difficult to explain
- Stakeholders didn't understand what was happening
- The work looked messy, ambiguous, or slow

The Double Diamond provided designers with a shared language for work that had previously been difficult to explain or legitimise.

A Different Starting Point

ITSM, by contrast, developed under very different conditions.

Where design struggled with ambiguity, ITSM was shaped by scale, risk, and operational dependency.

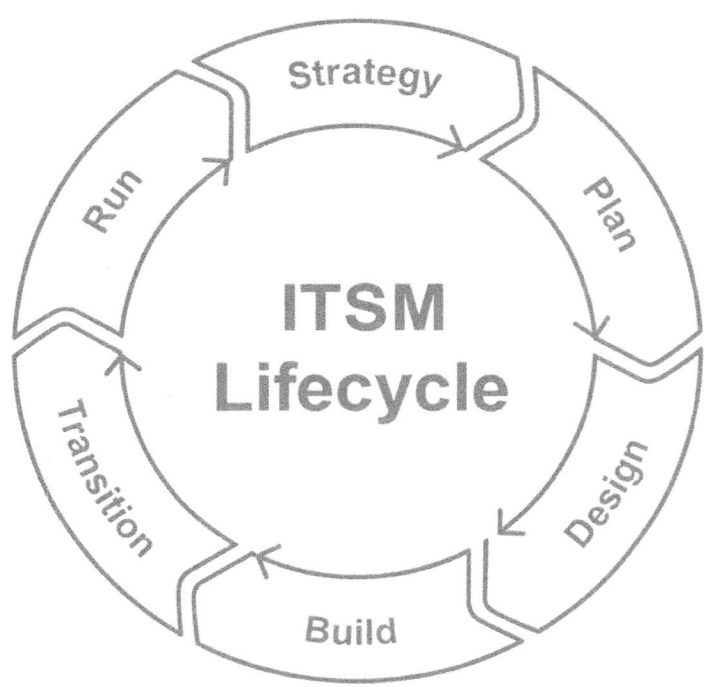

Figure 2: ITSM Lifecycle

This lifecycle:

- Emphasises stability, governance, accountability, and repeatability
- Provides structured mechanisms for decision-making once direction and priorities are established
- Focuses on managing services across their lifecycle to ensure reliability and control

Introducing the HIT DDF™

> *It is worth noting that the ITSM lifecycle is not owned by any single framework.*
>
> *While ITIL popularised one of the most widely recognised versions, the idea of a service lifecycle predates ITIL and appears in multiple forms across service management practice.*

These strengths have been central to IT's ability to operate at scale.

Introducing the HIT DDF™

How ITSM Came to Be

The ITSM lifecycle provides clarity about how work progresses once direction has been set. While it includes mechanisms for refining and reviewing decisions, it is primarily optimised for managing services after priorities have been agreed and work is ready to move forward.

The Double Diamond, however, begins earlier.

It focuses on the work that happens *before* commitment, when the nature of the problem itself is still uncertain, contested, or incomplete. It formalises a principle long understood in design practice: effective solutions depend on a deep understanding of the environment in which they will operate.

This difference does not reflect a weakness in ITSM. It reflects the fact that the discipline was never designed to answer certain questions.

The Space the Lifecycle Does Not Cover

In many organisations, requirements gathering is treated as the point at which understanding begins.

By that stage, key assumptions may already be locked in.

> *Requirements play a vital role in service design, but they typically emerge once a problem has already been articulated.*

The Double Diamond reduces the risk of well-executed solutions being applied to poorly understood problems.

As technology became embedded in everyday work, this gap became increasingly visible. Experience, behaviour, and context began to directly influence service outcomes, not as secondary considerations, but as operational realities.

The Missing Diamond

In ITSM environments, there is a strong and understandable tendency to move quickly toward action. Operational pressure, accountability, and risk management often reward decisiveness. Over time, this can lead to what is commonly described as *jumping into solution mode* — where attention shifts to tools, fixes, or implementations before the underlying problem has been fully understood.

Diamond One interrupts this pattern. It creates deliberate space for understanding to emerge before assumptions, inherited practices, or predefined solutions shape decisions. It is about ensuring effort is directed at the right problem.

The two diamonds guard against two different risks:

- Solving the wrong problem
- Choosing the wrong solution

Why ITSM Needed Its Own Version

Applied directly to ITSM, the Double Diamond lacks the structural safeguards required for enterprise realities.

The original Double Diamond was created for design-led disciplines. It was not designed to operate inside mission-critical environments shaped by governance, regulation, legacy systems, and operational risk.

At its core, the Double Diamond is a **sense-making model**, not an operating model.

It was created to:

- Legitimise exploration
- Establish a shared language for ambiguous work
- Support the framing and reframing of problems

It was not designed to:

- Manage enterprise risk
- Handle regulatory compliance
- Govern funding and approval mechanisms
- Operate at scale across complex service ecosystems
- Ensure operational continuity

Introducing the HIT DDF™

The HIT DDF™ ™ translates the intent of the Double Diamond into a form that can operate within ITSM, preserving human-centred design while embedding it inside the governance, accountability, and operational discipline required to run technology-enabled services at scale.

The Framework Behind Humanising IT™

We can now introduce the HIT DDF™, the core of Humanising IT™, the foundation of this book, and the framework through which a new way of thinking about ITSM is explored.

The HIT DDF™ is a structured system of activities that integrates human-centred design practices into the ITSM lifecycle, enabling IT teams to design experience-led services and processes within enterprise constraints.

The framework consists of:

- **Four design phases**, aligned to both the British Design Council Double Diamond and the ITSM lifecycle
- **Two diamonds** one to understand the right problem, and one to shape the right solution
- **Twenty-two structured activities**, distributed across those phases
- **Maintain / Run**, an additional phase where services are operated, supported, and experienced over time

The diagram below provides a high-level illustration of the HIT DDF™. It shows how the two diamonds align with the British Design Council, how the Maintain/Run phase extends the framework, and how ITSM lifecycle activities map to each phase of the Double Diamond model (explored later in this chapter).

Introducing the HIT DDF™

The activities for each diamond are outlined beneath the diagram.

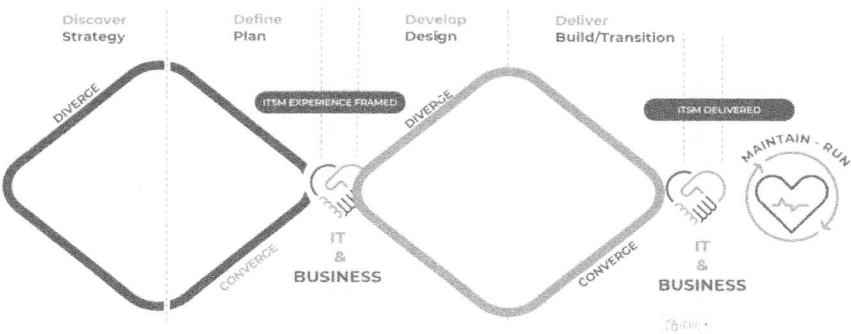

Figure 3: HIT DDF™

Activities Across the HIT DDF™

Discover / Strategy

Starting with the RIPP Trigger this phase is about understanding what is really happening, before deciding what to do

The goal is not to validate a solution, but to surface how the situation is being perceived, assumed, experienced, and navigated across the system.

Activities typically include:

1. **RIPP**

    Surfaces how a problem (the **RIPP Trigger**) is initially perceived by different stakeholders across the organisation.

2. **Assumptions Analysis**

    Identifies why stakeholders perceive the problem in the way they do.

3. **Experience Archetypes**

    Reveals recurring patterns of behaviour that emerge as people navigate the service under real conditions.

Introducing the HIT DDF™

4. **Research: Desktop**

    Examines existing artefacts, data, and documentation to understand how the service is intended to operate.

5. **Research: Service Safari**

    Explores how the service is actually experienced by immersing in the context and observing how people interact with it.

6. **Experience Flow Sketching**

    Maps how experiences unfold over time, highlighting friction, decision points, and workarounds.

7. **Design vs Reality Review**

    Compares documented design intent with lived operational reality to expose gaps and misalignment.

8. **Moments that Matter**

    Identifies the points in the experience where outcomes, emotions, or trust are most strongly shaped.

9. **HIT Insight Briefing**

    Synthesises insights into a shared understanding that informs decisions in the next phase.

Define / Plan

Establishing clarity before design begins

This phase deliberately converges. The organisation moves from broad understanding to a shared, evidence-based focus.

Activities typically include:

10. **Empathy Mapping**

    Organising evidence to make lived experience explicit and shared.

11. **Insight Synthesis**

    Working across findings to identify what is shaping behaviour and why.

12. **Problem Framing**

    Articulating the tension between system design and lived reality.

13. **How Might We**

    Opening the opportunity space without collapsing into solutions.

14. **Prioritisation & Alignment Workshop**

    Agreeing where effort should be directed next.

At the close of this phase, IT and the business are aligned around what problem is worth solving — and why.

Develop / Design

Exploring and shaping possible responses

This phase re-opens divergence; exploration is guided by clarity grounded in evidence.

Activities typically include:

15. **Ideation**

    Generating possible ways to respond to the reframed problem.

16. **Low Fidelity Prototyping**

    Making ideas tangible enough to discuss and test.

17. **Co-design and User Experience Testing**

    Exploring concepts with the people who will live with the service.

18. **Iteration & Refinement**

    Narrowing options based on learning, not preference.

19. **Opportunity Alignment Workshop**

    Agreeing which concept is worth taking forward.

Introducing the HIT DDF™

Deliver / Build / Transition

Proving the service will work in the real world

This phase converges again. Ideas stop being ideas.

Activities typically include:

20. **Experience Validation & Refinement**

    Testing the service in realistic conditions with real roles and constraints.

21. **Technical Build**

    Configuring, building, and integrating the solution.

22. **System-Level Testing and Validation**

    Ensuring the service works end-to-end in its operating environment.

23. **Release Readiness**

    Ensuring readiness across roles, support, and governance before go-live.

This last phase is about making the service real, stable, and ready for the organisation.

Maintain / Run

Where design meets reality, continuously

Maintain / Run is not a fifth phase.

It is the environment in which everything designed is tested, stressed, adapted, and either reinforced or undermined.

In Humanising IT™, Maintain/Run is not the end of the design conversation.

Maintain / Run is where experience becomes visible at scale and this is how Humanising IT™ treats experience: as part of the operating logic and rhythm of ITSM.

Introducing the HIT DDF™

> *This book does not teach every activity in full. Instead, it focuses primarily on* **Diamond One** *of the HIT DDF™ — the part of the framework where ITSM gains the greatest leverage by strengthening how problems are explored, understood, and framed before decisions are made.*
>
> **Diamond Two** *— where solution options are developed, tested, and prepared for delivery — is already deeply embedded within the ITSM lifecycle. The intent of this book is not to replace those practices, but to complement them by strengthening the thinking that informs them.*
>
> *Accordingly, this book provides the context for why the activities in the HIT DDF™ exist, what they reveal, and how they change the way IT thinks, plans, and designs — leaving detailed application and facilitation to Humanising IT™ training and certification.*

Same Outcome Different Models

When the Double Diamond is placed alongside the ITSM lifecycle, their structural similarities become apparent. Both follow a progression from early exploration through to design, build, and delivery.

As I brought the two models together, a clear pattern emerged. The stages were not competing with one another; they were aligned in intent, but expressed through different disciplines and language.

This raised a familiar question:

Why had these models remained separate for so long?

Viewed together, the alignment becomes clear:

- **Discover** aligns with **Strategy** — supporting exploration of context, intent, and the environment in which services must operate
- **Define** aligns with **Plan** — helping converge on the right problem and inform clear direction

- **Develop** aligns with **Design** — exploring and testing solution approaches before commitment
- **Deliver** aligns with **Build / Transition** — building, implementing, validating, and preparing services for use

These alignments reflect *when* different types of thinking occur, not how governance, risk, or accountability are managed. The Double Diamond contributes sense-making and problem clarity; the ITSM lifecycle provides the controls required to act on those decisions.

A further insight emerged. While the Double Diamond concludes at delivery, ITSM begins some of its most critical work at that point.

By explicitly extending the design journey beyond delivery, the HIT DDF™ recognises that experience is not fixed at launch, but formed through day-to-day operation, support, and ongoing decisions — in other words, through ITSM.

This is reflected in an additional phase of the HIT DDF™:

- **Maintain / Run** — where services are operated, supported, adapted, and experienced over time.

This extension anchors experience within the operational reality of ITSM, where services succeed or fail over time.

Where We Go Next

The next section of this book turns from framework logic to practice, focusing on Diamond One, where ITSM has traditionally had the least explicit structure. We begin with the first activity in the HIT DDF™: **RIPP — Recognising the Initial Perceived Problem.**

Chapter 5

Diamond One – Phase 1

Discovery/Strategy: Understanding the Problem

This chapter explores the activities within the Discover / Strategy phase of the HIT DDF™. These activities form the first phase of Diamond One and are designed to help IT teams understand how a situation is initially perceived by different stakeholders, before decisions are made or solutions are shaped.

In human-centred design, **Discover** is about opening up the problem space. It focuses on surfacing perceptions, perspectives, and early signals without attempting to define the problem too quickly.

> ### *What "Sense-Making" Means*
>
> *Throughout this book you'll see terms commonly used in human-centred design. One of these is sense-making. We use it often, so it's worth being clear about what it means.*
>
> **Sense-making is the process of turning information into understanding.**
>
> *It's what teams do after gathering evidence but before deciding what the problem is or what to do about it.*

In ITSM, **Strategy** plays a complementary role. It establishes the context in which services operate, including organisational goals, constraints, risks, and priorities. Strategy determines what is paid attention to, what is measured, and what is treated as legitimate concern.

The HIT DDF™ brings these two lenses together. Discover / Strategy creates a pause before action, allowing IT teams to surface perceptions, assumptions, and early patterns of behaviour within the strategic context in which the service operates.

The activities that support this phase are outlined below and explored in the sections that follow.

Discover/Strategy Activities

1. **RIPP**

   Surfaces how a problem (the **RIPP Trigger**) is initially perceived by different stakeholders across the organisation.

2. **Assumptions Analysis**

   Identifies why stakeholders perceive the problem in the way they do.

3. **Experience Archetypes**

   Reveals recurring patterns of behaviour that emerge as people navigate the service under real conditions.

4. **Research: Desktop**

   Examines existing artefacts, data, and documentation to understand how the service is intended to operate.

5. **Research: Service Safari**

   Explores how the service is actually experienced by immersing in the context and observing how people interact with it.

6. **Experience Flow Sketching**

   Maps how experiences unfold over time, highlighting friction, decision points, and workarounds.

7. **Design vs Reality Review**

   Compares documented design intent with lived operational reality to expose gaps and misalignment.

8. **Moments that Matter**

    Identifies the points in the experience where outcomes, emotions, or trust are most strongly shaped.

9. **HIT Insight Briefing**

    Synthesises insights into a shared understanding that informs decisions in the next phase.

How Discover Aligns With Strategy in ITSM

In traditional ITSM, *Strategy* is the stage where the organisation seeks to understand demand, clarify business needs, and determine where attention and investment should be directed. It is the space where IT steps back from solutions and asks the more fundamental question: **What truly matters, and why?**

The Discover phase in the HIT DDF™ aligns directly with this intent — but deepens it.

Where ITSM Strategy focuses on understanding business objectives and service demand, HIT Discover focuses on understanding the **human context** behind that demand: the behaviours, constraints, pressures, workarounds, and moments that shape how people actually experience IT services.

Both phases share the same purpose:

- Understand the problem before defining it
- Surface the real sources of demand
- Uncover what is meaningful to the organisation
- Avoid premature solutioning

The difference is emphasis.

ITSM Strategy identifies what the business needs.

HIT Discover uncovers **why** those needs exist and **how** they manifest in real environments.

By aligning these two perspectives, IT gains a more complete foundation for decision-making: not just what the business wants, but what people actually do, struggle with, and rely on. This ensures that the opportunities selected in Diamond One are grounded in reality, not assumptions.

Activity 1: RIPP: Recognising the Initial Perceived Problem

Why the Same Situation Produces Multiple, Coexisting Truths

Problems in ITSM rarely arrive naked.

They arrive already clothed, wrapped in interpretation, urgency, and prior judgement. By the time an issue reaches a steering group, a backlog, or a decision forum, it has usually been named, framed, and prioritised based on how it was first encountered.

Those clothes matter.

They are shaped by role, proximity to the work, operational pressure, incentives, and accountability. What one group experiences as a technical failure may already be dressed by another as a process breakdown, a capacity issue, or a risk exposure.

> *By the time an initiative is proposed or a decision is required, the "problem" has often been named with confidence and urgency.*

Each version can feel complete.

Each can feel true.

These versions are not reality itself, they are perceptions of reality.

And once articulated, those perceptions begin to drive action.

This is how a single situation produces multiple, co-existing truths in ITSM, not because anyone is wrong, but because the problem was never neutral to begin with.

In this way, the RIPP Trigger marks the formal starting point of Diamond One: not when a solution is proposed, but when a **perceived** problem first enters the system as something to be acted upon.

This is where Humanising IT™ introduces RIPP.

Diamond One – Phase 1

> ## *A recurring scenario*
>
> A service desk is experiencing a sustained increase in escalations to senior executives. Incidents that would traditionally remain within operational channels are being raised informally, bypassing agreed processes. Senior leaders are frustrated. IT leadership is under pressure to act.
>
> From this point, a familiar sequence begins. Options are discussed: extending service desk hours, increasing vendor capacity, revisiting escalation rules, or renegotiating contracts.
>
> At their core, each option reflects a perception of escalation.

Perception as Survival Mechanism

Perception is not a flaw in human reasoning. It is a survival mechanism. Faced with overwhelming amounts of information, the brain continuously selects what feels relevant, suppresses what feels peripheral, fills gaps with prior experience, and constructs a story coherent enough to support action. Without this process, decision-making would be impossible.

However, this efficiency comes at a cost.

Two people can encounter the same situation and sincerely describe entirely different problems, not because one is mistaken, but because each is seeing through a different perceptual frame.

A Simple Illustration of Perception

Figure 4: Rabbit–Duck Illusion

Most people see either a rabbit or a duck first.

Nothing in the image changes.
Only the frame applied by the viewer.

Once one interpretation becomes dominant, it is remarkably difficult *not* to see it. The alternative does not disappear, it simply recedes from awareness. This phenomenon is not visual trivia; it is an illustration of how meaning is constructed in everyday organisational life.

Diamond One – Phase 1

Different Roles, Different Signals?

Perception in organisations is rarely shaped solely by individual preference or personality. It is shaped by role.

People interpret situations through the responsibilities they are accountable for, the risks they are exposed to, and the outcomes they are expected to protect. Over time, professional roles train attention, teaching people what to notice, what to ignore, and what constitutes success or failure.[1]

People do not perceive "the problem."
They perceive the problem as it appears from where they stand.

- A cybersecurity professional is trained to see exposure.
- A service manager is trained to see stability.
- A frontline worker is trained to see interruption.
- An executive is trained to see consequence.

This is not bias in the moral sense. It is structured sense-making.

The Illusion of a Single, Objective Problem

Many organisational disciplines including ITSM are highly effective when problems are technical in nature. A server outage, a failed component, or a broken dependency can often be named, isolated, and resolved with precision.

Human-shaped problems do not behave this way.

They do not arrive neatly labelled.
They do not have a single point of origin.
They are experienced differently depending on role, proximity, and pressure.

Yet organisations frequently treat the *first articulation* of a problem as if it were an objective description of reality. Once that framing takes hold,

---

[1] This idea is grounded in organisational research commonly referred to as *role identity theory*, which examines how professional roles shape interpretation, behaviour, and decision-making.

everything that follows — analysis, planning, tooling decisions, automation, even AI implementation becomes anchored to that initial interpretation.

This is where many well-intentioned IT initiatives quietly derail.

From Perception Theory to RIPP in Practice

In organisational settings, the same perceptual dynamics apply.

Each interpretation is coherent within its own frame of reference. Each reflects what that role is trained to notice, prioritise, and act upon. And, as with the rabbit–duck image, once a particular interpretation takes hold, alternative readings become less visible, not because they are invalid, but because the cognitive task of sense-making has already been completed.

However, in complex service environments, this rapid closure has a consequence. Early problem descriptions begin to function as if they were objective representations of the system, rather than partial interpretations shaped by position, accountability, and context. Subsequent decisions — planning, tooling, escalation paths, automation, and governance responses — then become anchored to that initial framing.

At this stage, the question is not whether the problem description is "correct" or "incorrect". The more relevant question is what has been made visible and what has been rendered invisible by the way the situation has been framed.

The RIPP Trigger

Rather than treating the first articulation of a problem as a stable point of reference, the HIT DDF™ treats it as a signal.

This signal is referred to as the **RIPP Trigger**.

The RIPP Trigger is when a situation is framed as a "problem" and presented for action, often through escalation, incident trends, executive concern, operational pressure, or repeated dissatisfaction. It may appear as a statement such as:

- "The service desk is overwhelmed."
- "Escalations are increasing."
- "Users are not following the process."
- "The system is unreliable."
- The vendor is not meeting contractual obligations
- "We need automation."

At this point, something important has already occurred: the situation has been interpreted. Meaning has been assigned. A narrative has begun to form about what the problem is and where it resides.

RIPP In Practice

In its simplest form, RIPP is a short, structured sense-making activity. It is often run as an informal working session with key stakeholders, focused on a single question:

What do you believe triggered this problem?

The intent is not to judge, debate, or resolve differing views. There is no attempt to validate assumptions, propose solutions, or reach agreement.

RIPP surfaces how the problem is currently being perceived across the organisation by different stakeholders.

That visibility prepares for the next activity in the HIT DDF™: Assumptions Analysis, where the focus shifts from *what* people perceive to *why* those perceptions exist.

Activity 2: Assumptions Analysis

Why People Believe What They Believe

If RIPP helps us see how different roles perceive the same situation, Assumptions Analysis helps us understand **why** those role-shaped interpretations feel true.

In ITSM, assumptions are rarely experienced as assumptions. They are experienced as reality.

This is not because IT professionals are unreflective or resistant to change. It is because the assumptions shaping ITSM are rarely personal beliefs. They are structural, inherited through frameworks, tooling, governance, training, and decades of professional reinforcement.

Most assumptions in ITSM do not present themselves as opinions that can be debated.

They present themselves as:

- Educated truths
- Responsible behaviour
- Best practice
- "How competent IT works"

"Our job is to restore services. We don't fix the root cause.
Statements like this are rarely experienced as assumptions. **They are treated as professional fact.**

This is precisely what makes them so difficult to see.

When an idea is embedded in guidance, encoded in process models, reinforced by tooling, validated through audits, examined through certification, and rewarded through metrics, it no longer feels provisional.

It feels proven.

It feels like the natural order of things.

Over time, assumptions stop sounding like interpretations of how work *might* happen.

They begin to sound like descriptions of how work *does* happen.

Assumptions Are Not a Failure of Thinking

If perception explains how individuals make sense of complexity, assumptions explain how organisations stabilise that sense-making over time.

Assumptions should not be treated as a weakness.
In fact, assumptions are how complex socio-technical systems remain workable at scale.

Without them:

- Every decision would require re-examination
- Every action would stall under uncertainty
- Every workflow would collapse under analysis

Assumptions enable speed, coordination, and consistency across large, distributed environments. They are not the enemy of professionalism; they are one of its foundations.

The problem is not that assumptions exist.
The problem is that assumptions often remain invisible long after the conditions that made them useful have changed.

When Bias Is Built Into the System

Once assumptions are embedded, they begin to shape how information is interpreted. This is where bias enters ITSM, as structured sense-making.

One of the most influential forms is **confirmation bias**: the tendency to favour information that reinforces what already feels true, while discounting signals that challenge it.

> *In ITSM,* **confirmation bias rarely appears overt or unreasonable***. It is often reinforced through what are widely accepted as good practice.*

For example:

- **Incidents are restored quickly and then handed to a separate process**, reinforcing the assumption that understanding the underlying cause can be deferred to another role with different priorities.
- **Processes are documented, updated, and rolled out**, with the assumption they will be read, circulated, and understood as intended.
- **Knowledge is captured and published**, with the assumption that people will find it at the moment of need and apply it correctly.
- **Escalation paths are defined**, with the assumption that real-world situations will follow those paths cleanly under pressure.

None of these assumptions are irrational. They are coherent within the logic the system has normalised through frameworks, training, certification, and organisational reinforcement. Over time, that coherence makes them feel self-evident, and therefore difficult to question.

From Perception to Assumption

In the first activity of the HIT DDF™ - **RIPP,** we pause to look at how a situation is currently being described across the system.

RIPP does not ask whether those descriptions are right or wrong. It simply makes visible the different ways the same situation is being perceived, shaped by role, proximity to the work, operational pressure, and accountability.

Assumptions Analysis follows from this. It shifts the focus from *what* people perceive to *why* those perceptions make sense to them — not as individual opinions, but as conclusions shaped by experience, structure, and the environment they operate within.

Where RIPP surfaces perception, Assumptions Analysis examines what sits beneath it.

A Simple Example Outside of IT

Imagine a front door found open late at night.

Several people notice it.

Nothing about the physical situation differs. The door is open. That is the observable fact. Yet almost immediately, **perception** begins.

Step 1: Perception

(What each person makes of what they observe)

- The mother perceives an oversight.
- The father perceives a security risk.
- The teenager perceives an environmental cause.
- The neighbour perceives atypical activity.

Each person has observed the same thing: The door is open.

But perception is already different.
Not because the facts differ, but because meaning has been assigned.

Step 2: Assumption

(Why each person believes it happened)

- The mother assumes someone simply forgot to close it.
- The father assumes someone may have entered the house.
- The teenager assumes the wind blew it open.
- The neighbour assumes the delivery person earlier may be responsible.

These assumptions are not random.

They are shaped by role, responsibility, experience, and perceived risk.

They matter, because assumptions determine action.

One person closes the door.

Another checks the locks.
Another does nothing.
Another alerts someone else.

The behaviour follows the assumption, not the perception.

The Same Pattern Inside IT

Return to the service desk escalation scenario.

Escalations are increasing. Issues that would normally remain within operational channels are being raised informally. Senior leaders are frustrated. IT leadership is under pressure to act.

The **RIPP Trigger** is shared across the organisation.

The perceptions and assumptions formed in response to it are not.

Step 1: Perception

(How the RIPP Trigger is being interpreted)

- Operations perceive rising queues, slower resolution times, and increased handoffs.
- Security perceives consistent enforcement of controls and increased security-related checks.
- The service desk perceives more incidents escalating beyond first-line support.
- Executives perceive delays in delivery and growing noise around IT performance.

Each group is responding to the same situation.
Perception has already diverged.

Step 2: Assumption

(Why each group believes it is happening)

- Operations assume the environment is under-provisioned.
- Security assumes controls are correctly designed and behaving as intended.

Diamond One – Phase 1

- The service desk assumes instability is originating from upstream change or transition.
- Executives assume IT lacks agility, responsiveness, or operational maturity.

> Whichever assumption dominates will determine what is prioritised, funded, and addressed.

Each assumption is logical within its own domain, but none describe the whole system.

Assumptions Analysis does not decide which explanation is correct. It makes visible why particular interpretations feel true, before they harden into direction.

What it does not yet show is how those assumptions translate into **patterns of behaviour** over time.

That is the role of **Experience Archetypes**, the next activity in the HIT DDF™ explored in the section that follows.

Diamond One – Phase 1

Activity 3: Experience Archetypes

How Behaviour Reveals the System You've Designed

How a system is experienced day to day is rarely shaped by who designed it or who approved it. Services may be formally documented, governed, and signed off by appropriate stakeholders. Workflows may be agreed. Controls may be in place.

But lived experience is shaped elsewhere, in the quiet, cumulative adaptations people make when systems meet real work.

Over time, organisations do not simply use IT services.
They **adapt** to them.

Those adaptations the workarounds, the escalations, the silence, the enforcement of rules — become the true operating model. They rarely appear in documentation. They are seldom discussed explicitly. Yet they determine whether a service feels usable, trustworthy, or safe.

This is where traditional ITSM design reaches its limit.

What Is an Archetype and Why Human-Centred Design Uses Them

In human-centred design, archetypes are used to describe **recurring patterns of behaviour, not individual people**. They help designers move beyond isolated examples to understand how systems consistently shape action under certain conditions.

Rather than personalising issues — *"that person is difficult," "this team resists change," "users don't follow process"* archetypes shift attention to **how people tend to respond** when faced with similar constraints, pressures, and incentives.

This allows behaviour to be examined as an outcome of design, context, and environment, rather than as a personal trait, capability, or attitude.

Within the HIT DDF™, they draw on insight IT already holds, often tacitly, from years of observing incidents, escalations, workarounds, and the hidden labour required to keep work moving.

Within human-centred design, archetypes are typically created after research. The HIT DDF™ differs by forming Experience Archetypes earlier, using existing operational insight to focus where research should look next.

Archetypes give designers a way to see patterns that would otherwise remain fragmented across roles, teams, or incidents. They make it possible to reason about behaviour at a system level, especially when the same workarounds, escalations, or adaptations appear again and again.

This is the lens the HIT DDF™ adopts through Experience Archetypes.

A Simple Example Outside IT

Consider ordering coffee.

The same café.

The same barista.

The same menu.

The same day.

Every customer has the same access.

They can order, pay, and wait.

Yet behaviour differs.

- One person wants speed. Minimal interaction. Order ahead and grab and go.
- Another wants recognition. The barista remembers yesterday's order.
- Another wants reassurance. Confirmation the order is correct.
- Another welcomes conversation. The interaction *is* part of the experience.

Nothing about the environment has changed.
Nothing about access has changed.
What differs is not identity, but behavioural pattern.

Designers understand this instinctively. They do not design cafés for personality types or demographics. They design for recurring patterns of behaviour that reliably appear under the same conditions.

A Simple Example Inside IT

Consider a standard IT service desk portal.

The same portal.
The same service desk.
The same services available.
The same day.
Every user has the same access.

They can log an incident, request support, or check status.

Yet behaviour differs.

- One user logs a ticket and waits patiently, trusting the process to work.
- Another logs a ticket and immediately follows up with an email or message "just to be sure."
- Another bypasses the portal entirely and contacts someone they know to speed things up.
- Another escalates early, not because the issue is severe, but because past experience suggests delays.

Nothing about the system has changed.
Nothing about access has changed.

What differs is **how people behave** under the same conditions.

These recurring responses are not random. They emerge consistently when people operate within the same system, under similar pressures, expectations, and constraints.

Within the HIT DDF™ these recurring patterns are what we refer to as **Experience Archetypes** and is the third activity in the HIT DDF™.

Roles Define Permission — Not Behaviour

Let's now turn our attention to how ITSM is typically designed.

ITSM is built on roles.
Users request services.
Administrators configure systems.
Approvers authorise change.
Read-only roles observe but do not act.

These roles are essential.

They define access, authority, and responsibility within the system.
Processes assume them.
Tools enforce them.
Governance depends on them.

Roles explain **what someone is allowed to do** —

not **how they behave when the system meets real work.**

People do not interact with IT services as job titles.
They interact as humans trying to get work done under varying levels of pressure, risk, time constraint, and consequence.

The same person may behave very differently depending on what is at stake.

Changing the Design

Experience Archetypes reveal how people actually respond when they must keep work moving — how they adapt, cope, escalate, endure, bypass, or enforce rules in practice.

Most importantly, they prevent research from starting with premature solutions framed as questions, such as:

1. What process needs stronger enforcement?
2. What controls need tightening?
3. What training needs refreshing?

Diamond One – Phase 1

4. What guidance needs clearer communication?

> *Experience Archetypes ensure that research does not begin by asking how to correct behaviour, but by seeking to understand how behaviour is emerging.*

These questions are understandable.

They start from the belief that the system is broadly correct and that the issue sits in execution.

When research begins from this position, future effort is quietly steered toward confirming that belief. Archetypes interrupt this default framing.

The guiding question becomes:

What is this system making it *reasonable* for people to do?

Archetypes do not answer it. They help IT decide where to look, what to observe, and what not to take for granted.

This is why Experience Archetypes come before research in the HIT Double Diamond™.

They prevent investigation from starting without a working view of behavioural patterns.

Reasonable Does Not Mean Right

You may have noticed the earlier question: "What is this system making it reasonable for people to do?

It's worth pausing on that word — reasonable — because it has a specific meaning in this context.

"Reasonable" is often misunderstood as "acceptable" or "justified".

That is not how the term is used here.

A behaviour can be entirely reasonable *and still problematic.*

- Escalating an issue may be reasonable when feedback is slow, even if it undermines process.
- Working around a system may be reasonable when formal pathways add friction even if it introduces risk.
- Remaining silent may be reasonable when raising issues has previously delivered no value — even if it hides impact.

Humanising IT™ does not excuse, judge or condone these behaviours.

It seeks to understand why they persist.

Why Archetypes Are Not Personas

Experience Archetypes are not personas.

They do not describe **who** someone is.
They describe **how** someone behaves when interacting with a system under particular conditions.
Most importantly, archetypes are **situational**, not fixed.
The same person may move between archetypes depending on pressure, timing, risk, and consequence.

This is the same pattern seen in the coffee example.

The same person may visit the same café on different days and behave differently. One day they want speed and minimal interaction. Another day they welcome conversation. Nothing about the person has changed. What has changed is context, pressure, and intent in that moment.

The same dynamic appears in ITSM. The same person responding differently as conditions change:

In a low-impact situation, the person logs a ticket and follows process
In a time-critical or high-risk situation, the same person bypasses process and escalates

These differences are not personality traits or role issues. They are **context-driven responses**.

This is why Humanising IT™ uses Experience Archetypes early in the HIT DDF™. Archetypes allow teams to understand what behaviour is occurring and why, without labelling, stereotyping, or blaming people.

Personas — which focus on people rather than behaviour — are introduced later, once patterns are understood and the work moves toward framing problems and making decisions.

That fluidity is precisely what makes Experience Archetypes useful, and why they are adopted within the HIT DDF™ as a foundation for understanding experience in ITSM.

Introducing the Five Humanising IT™ Experience Archetypes

Humanising IT™ includes five core Experience Archetypes, behavioural patterns that have emerged consistently across years of consulting, research, training, and real-world observation in IT environments around the world across many industries.

These archetypes were not created in theory.

They were shaped through thousands of hours spent:

- Inside service desks
- In operational war rooms
- In frontline environments
- In executive escalations
- In design workshops
- In organisations at every level of IT maturity

Across industries, cultures, and operating models, the same behavioural patterns appeared again and again — not because people are the same, but because **systems create predictable conditions**, and humans adapt to those conditions in predictable ways.

The five Humanising IT™ Experience Archetypes are:

- **Process Guardian/Rule Enforcer**
- **Escalator**
- **Silent Sufferer**
- **Workaround Expert**
- **Blame Shifter**

These archetypes are provided here and taught in depth through Humanising IT™ training as practical tools to help IT teams understand behaviour without personalising it.

Remember:

They are not personality types.
They are not labels for individuals.
They are not assessments of competence or intent.

They are **situational responses** to system design within in ITSM.

You may find that some archetypes appear more strongly in your organisation than others.
You may find that certain teams gravitate toward particular patterns.
You may even find that your culture amplifies or suppresses some behaviours.

But in our experience across hundreds of organisations these five archetypes appear with remarkable consistency. They provide a shared language for discussing behaviour *reasonable* as a response to conditions, rather than as a reflection of individual personality or motivation.

With that foundation in place, we can now explore the five archetypes in detail.

The following five archetypes represent the behavioural patterns most commonly seen when people adapt to IT systems under real conditions.

Process Guardian/Rule Enforcer

The Process Guardian/Rule Enforcer responds to uncertainty by holding tightly to structure.

When systems feel fragile, overloaded, or unpredictable, this archetype seeks safety in rules, procedures, and defined pathways. Consistency feels protective.

This behaviour often emerges in environments with regulatory pressure, audit exposure, or accountability without direct control. It is not driven by a desire to control others, but by a need to prevent the system from failing.

Signal: The system feels unsafe without rules.

Escalator

The Escalator responds to uncertainty by increasing visibility and authority.

When time, reputation, safety, or delivery feels threatened, this archetype bypasses standard pathways to regain control. Waiting feels riskier than acting. Escalation becomes rational when feedback is slow or outcomes are unclear.

This behaviour is often misread as impatience.
More often, it signals a lack of certainty at critical moments.

Signal: The system is not providing timely reassurance or clarity.

Silent Sufferer

The Silent Sufferer responds to friction by enduring it.

They adapt quietly, absorb disruption, and avoid raising issues unless absolutely necessary. Asking for support feels costly. Past experiences may have reduced trust. The process may feel harder than the problem itself.

From IT's perspective, this archetype is often invisible.

Signal: Effort has shifted from the system onto people — and impact is being hidden.

Workaround Expert

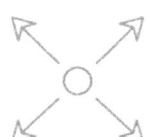

The Workaround Expert responds to system friction with ingenuity.

They find shortcuts, share unofficial fixes, and keep work moving despite the system. Outcomes matter more than compliance. Progress matters more than process.

This behaviour is often praised because work gets done.

But workarounds carry hidden cost: bypassed controls, inconsistency, and issues that never surface.

Signal: The system no longer fits the reality of the work.

Blame-Shifter

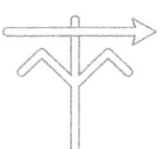

The Blame-Shifter responds to pressure by deflecting accountability.

When outcomes are judged harshly and failure carries consequence, this archetype focuses on proving where responsibility does not sit. Process, approvals, governance, and ownership boundaries become shields.

Signal: The system punishes failure more than it supports improvement.

Why Experience Archetypes Usually Stabilise at Four or Five

Many Roles, Few Behavioural Patterns

At first, it can feel implausible that a complex organisation could be meaningfully described through a small number of Experience Archetypes.

Consider a school.

There are principals, teachers, students, parents, administrative staff, and casual workers. Each group has different responsibilities, authority, access, and accountability. On the surface, their experiences appear too varied to be captured through a limited set of patterns.

But when attention shifts from **roles** to **behaviour**, something different becomes visible.

Take a familiar situation: contacting the service desk.

Across the school, emails begin to appear that are abrupt, impatient, or sharply worded. The underlying stories differ. A principal may be under time pressure. A teacher may be managing a classroom disruption. A casual staff member may be unsure how the system works. A junior administrator may be anxious about making a mistake.

The roles differ.
The pressures differ.
The context differs.
Yet the behaviour is the same.

The tone, urgency, and form of engagement follow a recognisable pattern that appears across seniority, responsibility, and access.

Instead of treating every incident, escalation, or complaint as unique, IT can now ask more experience-led questions about the conditions producing these patterns. That is the role of **Desktop Research**, where documented intent, design decisions, metrics, and system rules are examined to understand *why* these behaviours make sense within the current service design.

Research as a Foundation in Human-Centred Design

Human-centred design is grounded in evidence.

Its success comes not from understanding the environment in which people operate — the conditions, constraints, and expectations that shape behaviour.

In Humanising IT™, this principle is applied through two complementary research activities within the HIT DDF ™:

- **Desktop Research**
- **Service Safari**

Both are concerned with understanding context before change. The difference lies in *what* is examined first.

In the HIT DDF™, research begins with Desktop Research. This focuses on the documented intent of a service or process.

Only once this intent is understood does the framework move into Service Safari, where people are observed interacting with the service in real contexts.

This sequence matters.

Before interpreting behaviour, IT must first understand the system people are operating within. Doing so ensures that observation is grounded in intent rather than assumption, and that differences between design and reality can be examined with clarity rather than judgement.

The section that follows introduces the first of these activities: Desktop Research.

Activity 4: Research — Desktop

Research Begins with the System

Having surfaced how situations are perceived, why those perceptions feel reasonable, and how behaviour stabilises into recurring patterns, the HIT DDF™ now turns to research.

In ITSM, behaviour is never unconstrained. It is shaped by many artefacts including historical decisions that define what "good" work looks like and how work is expected to flow. Before attempting to understand how people behave within that environment, it is essential to understand how the environment itself has been designed.

> *ITSM artefacts do not describe what happens in practice. They describe what the organisation* **believes should happen.**

This is the role of Desktop Research.

Desktop Research focuses on the artefacts an organisation relies on to run its services. It draws on material the organisation already holds, including:

- Process documentation and workflow definitions
- Policies, standards, and controls
- Tickets, logs, and operational records
- Metrics, reports, and dashboards
- Escalation paths and decision thresholds

What Gets Measured — and the Assumptions Behind It

A phrase commonly attributed to Peter Drucker is often invoked in this context:

Diamond One – Phase 1

"What gets measured gets managed."

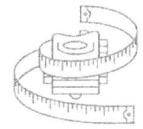
In ITSM, this idea has had significant influence. Metrics, KPIs, SLAs, and dashboards are frequently treated as objective indicators of service health. When the numbers appear acceptable, the service is assumed to be functioning as intended.

Humanising IT™ questions a quieter reality that often goes unexamined: that what is measured represents the full reality of the service.

Metrics are not neutral. They are the result of design choices, whether made deliberately or inherited over time.

What gets measured reflects what the organisation has decided matters.

Equally important is what has been excluded, simplified, or rendered invisible. Every metric carries embedded assumptions about behaviour, capability, motivation, time, risk, and compliance.

Rather than asking whether a metric is "right" or "wrong," Humanising IT™ asks different questions:

- What behaviour does this metric expect?
- What conditions does it assume people are operating under?
- What actions does it enable, constrain, or silently discourage?

Viewed this way, dashboards and reports become evidence of **design intent** — whether that intent was explicit or implicit.

Just as importantly, these artefacts reveal what sits outside that logic:

- Effort that never becomes a ticket
- Workarounds that prevent incidents from being logged
- Friction absorbed quietly so targets can still be met
- Behaviour that keeps work moving but never appears in a report

This means the data is partial, shaped by the design choices embedded in the system that produces it.

Where Experience Archetypes Re-Enter

This is where earlier work in the HIT DDF begins to converge.

At this stage, Experience Archetypes remain provisional. They are not validated, and they do not explain why behaviour occurs. Their role here is directional.

They provide a disciplined way to read existing artefacts.

Rather than treating ITSM artefacts as neutral descriptions, Desktop Research uses Experience Archetypes as a lens testing whether what the system expects aligns with the patterns already visible across the organisation.

This is where perception, assumptions, and early sense-making meet the documented system.

Using Archetypes as a Desktop Research Lens

When reviewing artefacts such as process documentation or survey questions, a designer does not ask:

- Is this process correct?
- Is this survey well designed?
- Are people following the steps?
- Is it aligned with best practice?

Instead, designers ask questions grounded in the Experience Archetypes already identified.

For example:

- Is the *Workaround Expert* likely to log an incident and bypass it to keep work moving?
- Is the *Blame Shifter* likely to engage with status updates
- Does this process assume the *Silent Sufferer* will raise issues proactively?

These question test whether the behavioural expectations encoded in the system are consistent with the behavioural hypotheses articulated through Experience Archetypes.

Scope of Desktop Research in This Book

Desktop Research can involve many artefacts: logs, tickets, dashboards, reports, policies, knowledge bases, metrics, and more. Most organisations are surrounded by documentation.

For the purposes of this book, the scope is deliberately narrowed. Not because other artefacts are unimportant but because attempting to cover everything would dilute the discipline this activity is designed to build.

This book focuses on two core artefacts only:

- **Process documentation**, which describes how work is meant to flow
- **Survey questions and measurement instruments**, which reveal what the organisation has chosen to measure and therefore manage

These artefacts are selected because they are:

- Widely available
- Familiar to ITSM professionals
- Rich in embedded behavioural assumptions

They allow us to ask: What view of behaviour does this artefact reflect and under what conditions is that behaviour expected to occur?

This shifts Desktop Research away from documentation review and toward behavioural insight. This approach applies regardless of artefact type.

Process Review

Process review in Humanising IT™ is not about checking compliance or confirming whether steps exist on paper. It is about examining what a process expects people to do, and the conditions under which those expectations are meant to hold.

Processes are written as if work unfolds in a stable, predictable way. In practice, they rely on a series of expectations about timing, access, clarity, and behaviour that are rarely made explicit. Reviewing a process through an experience lens helps surface those expectations before treating the process as a reliable reflection of reality.

The following example illustrates how this works in practice.

Example 1

Consider the common incident management step:

"Incident identified and logged."

For this step to function as designed, the system assumes that:

- The person believes logging will lead to action
- They are willing to interrupt their work
- They know where and how to log an incident
- They can describe the issue using the system's language
- They have the time, access, and capability to complete the process end to end
- They trust that logging is the correct starting point

Steps in the process reflect how IT expects work to occur, rather than how work is actually experienced.

Design insight:

The system treats ticket logging as the formal starting point for work.

This raises a critical question:

If logging is the only recognised starting point, **what happens to work that begins elsewhere?**

Example 2

Now consider another step widely used in incident management processes:

"IT provides a status update in the ticket."

On the surface, this appears to be a purely operational activity.
In practice, it embeds several behavioural assumptions.

For this step to function as intended, the system assumes that:

- The person waiting knows where to find the ticket and checks it regularly
- The meaning of each status label is understood without additional explanation
- A change in status is interpreted as evidence that progress is being made
- Reassurance can be delivered through status movement alone, without narrative or context
- Waiting for the next update is an acceptable and reasonable use of time

Diamond One – Phase 1

Design insight:

The system treats status movement as a proxy for progress.

Movement is easy to see. Progress is not.

Survey Review

We Examine the Question, Not the Response

In this activity, the HIT DDF™ does not analyse survey responses. Responses are shaped by timing, emotion, psychological safety, motivation, and willingness to participate. Those factors matter, but they belong later, during observation and inquiry.

Desktop Research focuses instead on the questions themselves.

Survey questions reveal what the organisation believes can be asked, measured, and compared.

They show how experience has been defined before anyone responds.

Survey Questions as Design Artefacts

☆☆☆☆☆
1 2 3 4 5

Example 1

"How satisfied were you with the incident resolution?"

The question assumes:

- a shared understanding of what "resolution" means
- sufficient recall of the experience
- comfort with translating experience into a score
- willingness to participate in formal feedback

These assumptions are not neutral.
They reflect how the organisation believes experience works and how it expects people to engage with the service.

Example 2

How was your experience?

This format appears modern, fast, and user-friendly.

But it encodes a very specific view of experience:

- That experience can be meaningfully reduced to approval or disapproval
- That ambivalence, trade-offs, or mixed outcomes do not matter
- That emotional response is more important than operational context
- That the moment of feedback reflects the whole experience

The gesture is simple.
The experience is not.

A user may give a thumbs up because the issue was eventually fixed — even if it took multiple attempts, workarounds, or personal escalation.

Another may give a thumbs down not because the service failed, but because the timing, pressure, or consequence made the disruption intolerable.

As with other feedback mechanisms, the format does more than capture sentiment.

It compresses experience into a binary signal, privileging speed of response over depth of understanding.

What cannot be expressed between thumbs up and thumbs down is unrepresented, despite often being critical to understanding how the service is experienced.

Crucially, while comments may allow some experiences to surface, the structure of the question still shapes what is measured, compared, and ultimately acted upon.

Diamond One – Phase 1

A Note on Survey Response Rates

Although this section focuses on survey questions as design artefacts, one issue cannot be ignored: **consistently low response rates**.

Across industries not just IT, survey participation is declining. Many organisations invest significant effort in designing questionnaires, only to hear from a small and often unrepresentative subset of users. Those who respond tend to be at the extremes: very satisfied, very dissatisfied, or unusually motivated to engage.

This creates a distorted picture of experience.

Low response rates do not mean people have nothing to say. More often, they reflect time pressure, survey fatigue, lack of trust that feedback will lead to change, or a mismatch between the questions asked and the realities people are navigating.

For this reason, Humanising IT™ is not an advocate of surveys as a primary measure of experience.

Surveys can have a place, but they are poorly suited to capturing the complexity, nuance, and context of how IT services are actually lived. They tend to measure what is easiest to ask and aggregate, rather than what is most meaningful to understand.

For this reason, Humanising IT™ does not treat surveys as a reliable standalone measure of experience.

What Desktop Research Can — and Cannot — Show

Desktop Research reveals how a service has been **designed to work**.

It makes visible the documented intent embedded in processes, metrics, dashboards, reports, and artefacts — what the system prioritises, how success is defined, and which behaviours are expected or rewarded.

What it cannot show is how that design is **experienced in practice**.

Documents do not reveal hesitation, improvisation, workarounds, or quiet effort.

Diamond One – Phase 1

Metrics do not show the judgement calls people make to keep work moving.

Dashboards do not capture what happens when reality does not fit the model.

At this point, the gap between **design intent** and **lived reality** is visible — but not yet understood.

To explore that gap, the HIT DDF™ now turns outward, away from documentation and into real environments.

This is the role of **Service Safari**, where services are observed as they are actually used, and where behaviour can be examined in context, rather than inferred from artefacts.

Activity 5: Service Safari

Seeing the Service as It Is Actually Experienced

Having examined how problems are perceived, why those perceptions exist, how behaviour stabilises into patterns, and the design intent of how services and process, the HIT DDF™ now turns to direct research.

This is the point at which inquiry moves beyond artefacts and into lived experience.

In human-centred design, this form of research is commonly referred to as a *service safari* — a practice used to understand how services are actually navigated in real conditions, rather than how they are intended to operate in theory.

Humanising IT™ adopts Service Safari to address a fundamental limitation in traditional ITSM: the tendency to infer experience indirectly, through tickets, metrics, surveys, and documentation.

Service Safari reintroduces direct engagement with the service as it is lived.

Service Safari: Where Written Design Meets Reality

In Humanising IT™, Service Safari is the deliberate observation of an IT service in use.

It focuses on how people interact with the service when work must continue under time pressure, uncertainty, interruption, and competing priorities.

Service Safari does not seek opinions, explanations, or preferences.
It does not begin with interviews or validation.
It begins with observation.

The intent is not to judge behaviour against process, but to understand how the service behaves when it meets real work.

Direct and Indirect Service Safari

Service Safari in Humanising IT™ can be conducted in two complementary ways.

Diamond One – Phase 1

Direct Service Safari

Involves experiencing the service first-hand working through the service exactly as users or staff are required to do

Designers move through the service as it is actually designed to be used

This may include:

- Admitting a patient
- Onboarding a new employee
- Setting up audio-visual equipment in a lecture hall before a class begins

Designers follow the same steps, rely on the same information, and encounter the same touchpoints and interactions as people using the service in the real world.

Indirect Service Safari

Involves observing work as it happens. Rather than asking people to explain what they do, practitioners spend time alongside them as they work — during busy periods, interruptions, and moments of pressure. The focus is on how services are really navigated when deadlines matter and consequences are real.

This may include:

- Sitting alongside service desk analysts
- Observing incident handling, escalation, and recovery
- Watching how tools, queues, and policies are navigated in real time
- Noticing interruptions, handovers, delays, and workarounds

By experiencing and seeing the service in motion, Humanising IT™ makes visible the reality of work as it is performed, not as it is documented.

Diamond One – Phase 1

Why Desktop Research Comes First

It is worth pausing briefly on the sequence of activities in the HIT DDF™. The order is deliberate.

Desktop Research helps teams see the system the behaviour is responding to. By reviewing processes, workflows, SLAs, escalation rules, and communication artefacts before observing work, the Humanising IT™ Practitioner ensures that behaviours are interpreted in relation to the design of the service — not as individual choices.

What looks like non-compliance often turns out to be the most reasonable way to get work done inside the system as designed.

The Role of Experience Archetypes during a Service Safari

In Humanising IT™, Experience Archetypes are introduced earlier than in traditional human-centred design. This is not because conclusions are reached sooner, but because IT already holds deep, tacit knowledge of recurring behavioural patterns formed through years of operational exposure.

At this stage, archetypes are treated as **provisional lenses**, not explanations. They guide attention during observation without assigning cause or meaning. Validation comes later, when observed behaviour, inquiry, and system evidence are considered together.

Consider a Humanising IT™ practitioner observing a service desk during a period of increased escalations.

Without archetypes, observation can quickly slide into interpretation:

- "That analyst is cutting corners."
- "That user is impatient."
- "This escalation is just bad behaviour."

With Experience Archetypes in mind, attention shifts:

- Escalations appear repeatedly when feedback is slow.
- Workarounds emerge when approval steps introduce delay.

- Silence follows incidents involving multiple handoffs.

Nothing is explained yet.

Nothing is judged.

The practitioner is simply noticing **which behaviours recur, and under what conditions**.

This is the discipline Experience Archetypes bring to Service Safari: They prevent early attribution and keep observation focused on patterns, not people.

Those observed patterns then become the foundation input for the next activity — Experience Flow Sketching — where behaviours are mapped across time to understand how effort, delay, uncertainty, and adaptation accumulate as work moves through the service.

Activity 6: Experience Flow Sketching

Seeing Experience Without Over-Engineering It

By this point in the HIT Double Diamond™, teams hold two essential perspectives:
what the service intent is(Desktop Research), and how it is actually lived and experienced (Service Safari).

Experience Flow Sketching brings these perspectives together visually. It is the first point at which design intent and lived experience are placed side by side — not to explain gaps or draw conclusions, but to make the flow of experience visible as it currently operates.

Experience Flow Sketching is deliberately low-fidelity. It captures the sequence of steps, decisions, handoffs, and friction points from the user's point of view, without requiring design skills or specialised tools.

In human-centred design, fidelity describes how closely something reflects real experience.

- Low-fidelity representations are rough and early.
  Sketches, whiteboards, simple walkthroughs, or role-plays.
  Their purpose is to explore direction, not detail.
- High-fidelity representations feel close to reality.
  They account for timing, pressure, handovers, interruptions, and real-world conditions.

Why We Don't Use Journey Mapping Here

Experience Flow Sketching is not journey mapping. It is a simpler, more disciplined precursor, designed specifically for ITSM contexts.

Journey mapping is a powerful design craft. When done well, it integrates interviews, emotional mapping, service touchpoints, backstage processes, and systemic dependencies across time, and typically represents a **high-fidelity view of experience**.

It also requires:

- Deep facilitation skill

Diamond One – Phase 1

- Careful synthesis of qualitative research
- Sustained organisational commitment
- And time that many IT teams simply do not have

Humanising IT™ respects journey mapping as a professional design discipline, but does not attempt to apply it in its pure form within the HIT DDF™. Instead, selected principles are adapted for use in practical, repeatable ways suited to most IT organisations.

The Core Structure of the Sketch

The Template

Teams typically sketch the experience using two simple columns:

1. Design Intent

What should have happened

- The official process
- The expected path
- The "happy flow" the system assumes

Figure 5: Experrence Flow Sketching

2. Lived Reality

What actually happened
- The real sequence of steps
- Workarounds, delays, and detours
- Emotional cues (confusion, frustration, relief)
- Escalations or shortcuts
- Behavioural patterns that explain why users act the way they do

This contrast is the heart of the activity

It makes the undocumented and invisible visible.

The Role of Experience Archetypes during Experience Flow Sketching

Experience Archetypes are **not** drawn into an Experience Flow Sketch as labels or overlays.

The sketch itself remains descriptive.

Its purpose is to capture what happens — the sequence of actions, decisions, delays, handoffs, interruptions, and adaptations that occur as work moves through the service.

Experience Archetypes are introduced **after** the sketch is complete.

They are used to interpret patterns across multiple flows, not to shape or constrain what is recorded in any single one.

In practice, this means:
- The sketch captures behaviour as it occurs
- Archetypes are used later to make sense of recurring behaviour across sketches

This separation matters.

By keeping archetypes out of the sketching activity itself, Humanising IT™ preserves analytical discipline. It prevents observers from forcing behaviour into predefined categories and ensures that patterns emerge from evidence, rather than being imposed by expectation.

Only once multiple flows have been examined does it become possible to see which Experience Archetypes are present, where they appear, and how consistently they recur.

This sequencing keeps Experience Flow Sketching grounded in observation — and Experience Archetypes grounded in synthesis.

Why Visual Sketching Matters

Visual sketching is one of several techniques Humanising IT™ adopts from human-centred design.

At this stage, Humanising IT™ uses visualisation instead of lengthy written documentation. This is not because documentation is unimportant, but because how humans process information matters when trying to understand complex services.

Reading a document is a sequential activity.

The reader must move line by line, hold information in working memory, and mentally reconstruct how steps, roles, and decisions relate to one another. In services involving multiple handoffs, queues, and exceptions, this quickly becomes cognitively demanding.

Visual sketching works differently.

By placing the whole experience in view at once, a sketch allows the brain to recognise patterns, relationships, and gaps without having to translate text into a mental model. Sequence, dependency, repetition, and divergence can be seen immediately — not inferred after the fact.

This difference matters.

Humans are significantly better at recognising structure, inconsistency, and flow when information is spatial rather than textual. Visualisation reduces cognitive load, allowing attention to be directed toward what is happening rather than decoding how it has been described.

Used this way, visual sketching:

Lowers the effort required to understand complex services

Allows multiple perspectives to be seen together without reconciliation

Makes misalignment visible without needing explanation

Reduces the urge to debate wording before understanding has formed

This is especially valuable in ITSM, where processes often appear coherent on paper but tell a very different story when actions, delays, workarounds, and lived experience are placed side by side.

Visual sketching does not replace documentation.

It precedes it, creating shared understanding before formalisation begins.

From Observation to Shared Reference

Experience Flow Sketching creates a visual anchor — a grounded, evidence-based depiction of how experience actually unfolds over time.

But the sketch is not the end of sense-making.

It is the point at which sense-making becomes shared.

Without a sketch:

- Discussion drifts into abstraction

- Stakeholders default to opinion or assumption

- Attention gravitates back to process rather than experience

With a sketch:

- Conversation is grounded in observable reality

- Stakeholders respond to something concrete

- The team gains a shared reference point for what *is*, not what is assumed

Experience Flow Sketching provides this shared reference.

The next activity in the HIT DDF™ — **Design vs Reality Review** — uses that reference to examine where documented design intent and lived experience diverge.

Together, these activities establish a concrete basis for alignment before decisions are made, solutions are shaped, or changes are approved.

Activity 7: Design vs Reality Review

Where Expectations Meet Experience

Every service contains two versions of itself:

- The version that is designed, documented, approved, and diagrammed
- The version that people actually experience

These two versions are rarely identical.

Over time, they drift. Assumptions age. Workarounds emerge. Teams adapt quietly to keep work moving. None of this indicates failure — it is simply how complex systems behave.

By this point in the HIT Double Diamond™, three perspectives are already in view:

1. **Desktop Research** has revealed what the system expects to happen.
2. **Service Safari** has shown what actually happens when people interact with the service.
3. **Experience Flow Sketching** has made that lived experience visible in a shared, concrete form.

The Design vs Reality Review brings these perspectives together.

Its purpose is not to decide what should change, but to surface where design intent and lived reality no longer align.

What This Activity Is

The Design vs Reality Review is a structured sense-making activity conducted by the design team.

Specifically, the review explores where system design intentions do not align with observed behaviour; which process steps or interactions generate friction, confusion, or workarounds; which assumptions are outdated, or unrealistic; which Experience Archetypes surface most clearly; and what the system implicitly treats as *"reasonable* behaviour" that lived reality does not consistently support.

What This Activity Is Not
- A process redesign
- A performance review
- A search for fault
- A debate about compliance

Humanising IT™ is not interested in whether people "follow the process."

It is interested in whether the process reflects the reality people must navigate.

A Lived Example: When Reality Wins

The official Change Management process required every change to include a risk score. The form offered clear criteria: impact, likelihood, complexity.

During the Design vs Reality Review, a pattern emerged.

When senior engineers submitted changes, the risk was almost always marked "Low," even when the work was complex. When newer staff submitted similar changes, the risk was marked "Medium" or "High," triggering extra approvals.

No one was gaming the system.

They were navigating it.

The design assumed risk scoring was objective.

Reality showed it was influenced by confidence, experience, and psychological safety.

The process wasn't broken, it simply didn't reflect how people actually assess risk under pressure.

Diamond One – Phase 1

Who Is Involved — and Why

The **Design vs Reality Review** is intentionally small and focused. It is conducted by the **design team** — the people directly involved in:

- RIPP and Assumptions Analysis
- Identification of Experience Archetypes
- Desktop Research
- Service Safari
- Experience Flow Sketching

Broader stakeholders are not involved at this stage. Their perspectives become valuable later, once the narrative is coherent and the insights are stable.

The review does not reopen debate about what the perceived problem is. It examines how the system as designed intersected with the reality made visible.

Activity 8: Moments That Matter

Why Certain Moments Shape the Entire Experience

By this point in the HIT DDF™, the design team has a clear view of the current state. The Design vs Reality Review has already surfaced where design intent and lived experience diverge.

What has not yet been made explicit is **where experience concentrates**.

Not every step in a service carries the same weight. Some interactions pass unnoticed. Others disproportionately shape how people interpret what is happening, how they remember the service, and how they decide what to do next. Activity 8 exists to identify those moments.

What a Moment That Matters Is

A Moment That Matters is not defined by process importance or operational effort.

It is defined by **human impact**.

It is a point in the experience where something shifts for the person involved — their understanding, their confidence, their sense of control, or their expectations of what will happen next.

In these moments:

What Moments That Matter Are Not

They are not the steps that are most visible, most operationally complex, or most resource-intensive.

A moment does not matter because the system considers it important. It matters because the person experiencing it does.

- Uncertainty increases or resolves
- Effort suddenly rises
- Trust is tested
- Behaviour adapts

A single interaction can quietly change how someone engages with the service from that point forward. The system may continue to function exactly as designed — but the experience has already been altered.

Why Human-Centred Design Focuses on Moments That Matter

Human-centred design uses Moments That Matter because experience is not evenly distributed across a service.

People do not remember every step.
They do not weigh every interaction equally.
They form judgement through a small number of moments where meaning concentrates.

Research in human-centred design consistently shows that people interpret an entire experience through a few key points — where effort spikes, uncertainty appears, control is lost or regained, or expectations shift. These moments disproportionately shape memory, trust, and future behaviour.

Designers therefore focus on **where experience is made**, not where process effort is highest.

This approach avoids a common failure mode in complex systems: trying to improve everything at once. When teams attempt to optimise entire journeys evenly, they dilute effort and miss the points that actually influence how the service is perceived and navigated.

By identifying Moments That Matter, human-centred design:

- Directs attention to the points that shape judgement
- Explains why people adapt, escalate, or disengage
- Reveals why technically "working" services still feel broken
- Creates leverage for meaningful improvement without redesigning everything

Humanising IT™ adopts this technique because ITSM environments are no different. Services may function correctly across dozens of steps, but experience often hinges on a few moments — where progress becomes unclear, responsibility feels ambiguous, or people must decide how to proceed.

Moments That Matter allow IT to see experience not as a full journey to perfect, but as a series of points where behaviour is shaped.

A Simple Example Outside of IT

Most of the car-rental experience is unremarkable.

You book online.
You arrive.
You sign paperwork.
You are handed keys.

But one moment dominates how the entire experience is remembered.

At the counter, the agent pauses and says:

"There's a small mark on the bumper. We'll note that."

That moment changes everything.

Suddenly, the customer:

- Pays closer attention
- Takes photos
- Rereads the contract
- Drives more cautiously
- Worries about being blamed

Nothing operationally complex has happened.
The system continues exactly as designed.

But trust, confidence, and perceived risk have shifted — and every interaction that follows is interpreted through that moment.

The bumper mark is not the most important step in the process.
It is simply the moment where meaning concentrates.

A Simple Example Inside of IT

An incident is logged.

The system works as designed:

- The ticket is created
- It enters the correct queue
- SLAs are active
- Engineers are investigating

For several hours, nothing changes from the user's perspective.

Then comes the moment that matters.

The user checks the portal.
The status still reads: **"In Progress."**
No update.
No explanation.
No indication of next steps.

At that point:
- Confidence drops
- Uncertainty rises
- The user stops trusting the process
- Escalation begins or workarounds form

Nothing has technically failed.
The incident is being worked.
The process is compliant.

But the experience has already turned.

That single moment — the absence of meaningful status — now defines how the service is judged, how IT is perceived, and how the user behaves next.

Why These Moments Matter

In both cases:
- The system is functioning
- The process is intact
- The failure is not technical

The experience shifts because of **how meaning is formed at a specific point**.

This is why design teams focuses on Moments That Matter to understand where experience is actually shaped.

Why Moments That Matter Lead to Insight

Identifying Moments That Matter does not produce solutions. It produces focus.

By this point, the design team is no longer dealing with a vague sense that "something isn't working." They can see **where experience concentrates**, where behaviour shifts, and where meaning is formed for the people using the service.

This prevents improvement work from spreading thinly across the entire journey or defaulting to what is most visible, loud, or easy to measure.

Instead, attention is directed to the moments that actually shape outcomes — operationally and experientially.

Moments That Matter provide the **raw material for synthesis**.

They give structure to what has been observed, surfaced, and sketched, and create the conditions for the next step in the HIT DDF™: turning insight into a clear, shared articulation of what matters for experience-led ITSM.

That work happens in the next activity: **HIT Insight Briefing**.

Activity 9: HIT Insight Briefing

Aligning on What Has Been Learned — Before Deciding What Comes Next

The HIT Insight Briefing marks the close of the Discover/Strategy phase in the HIT DD™.

It is the point where exploration stops expanding and learning is stabilised.

By this stage, the design team has already done the work:

- The initial perceived problem has been surfaced
- Underlying assumptions have been examined
- Recurring behavioural patterns identified through Experience Archetypes
- System intent understood through Desktop Research
- Lived experience observed through Service Safari
- Misalignment visualised through Experience Flow Sketching
- And interpreted through the Design vs Reality Review
- And the moments that carry disproportionate influence identified as Moments That Matter

What is needed now is not more data or deeper analysis, but **shared understanding**.

The HIT Insight Briefing ensures that what has been learned is made explicit and aligned before the organisation moves into problem definition, prioritisation, or solution design.

What This Activity Is

The HIT Insight Briefing is a structured conversation with key stakeholders to:

- Present the core insights emerging from the Discover / Strategy phase
- Articulate what the team now understands about the situation

It is not a workshop to generate new insight.

It is a briefing to consolidate and align on insight that has already been developed

What Is Presented

The briefing does not attempt to share all artefacts or research detail. Instead, it brings forward a small number of grounded, experience-led insights that explain:

- Where experience consistently breaks down
- How people are adapting to keep work moving
- Which system expectations no longer hold
- Where effort, risk, or cost is being absorbed by people rather than the system
- And why these patterns persist

These insights describe what is happening and why it matters — not what should be done.

Who Is Involved — and Why

Participants typically include people who own or govern the service, influence priorities, policy, or funding, define success measures, or will ultimately sponsor or enable change. For many of these stakeholders, this is the first time the service is presented as a coherent, end-to-end experience rather than as a set of reports, metrics, incidents, or escalations.

The intent is not to seek approval or endorsement, but to ensure that what has been learned is visible, shared, and understood by those whose decisions shape how the service operates.

Why This Activity Matters

Without a HIT Insight Briefing:

- Insight stays contained within the design team
- Stakeholders encounter findings piecemeal or reactively

- Problem definition becomes fragmented or political
- Solution work starts from misaligned assumptions

With it:

- Insight becomes organisational
- Decisions are grounded in evidence rather than opinion
- And the Define / Plan phase begins with coherence rather than contention

The HIT Insight Briefing is the point where learning becomes collective — and where the organisation is ready to decide what comes next.

Closing Out Phase One

The HIT Insight Briefing marks the close of Phase One of the HIT DDF™ — Discover / Strategy.

This phase has taken an experience-led approach while working directly with established ITSM processes, controls, and governance. Rather than abstracting from them, these structures have been engaged as they are designed to operate, providing a grounded view of the system in context.

Phase One establishes clarity about how design intent is expressed in practice — where it supports effective work, where it comes under pressure, and where people adapt to keep services moving.

By the end of this activity, the organisation holds a shared, evidence-based understanding of the current state of the service, shaped by both system design and lived experience.

With this foundation in place, the HIT Double Diamond™ moves into the Define / Plan phase — where decisions about focus, priorities, and change can be made with confidence, informed by insight rather than assumption.

Chapter 6

Diamond One – Phase 2

Define/Plan: Establishing Focus Before Design Begins

This chapter explores the activities within the Define / Plan phase of the HIT DDF™. These activities complete Diamond One and mark the transition from exploration to focus.

Where Discover / Strategy widened understanding, Define / Plan brings it into form. It is the phase where insight is consolidated, priorities are clarified, and direction is agreed before any design, build, or implementation decisions are made.

In this phase, IT teams work to:

- Articulate what is now understood about the problem space
- Distinguish signal from noise across the insights gathered
- Agree where attention should be directed
- Establish the boundaries and intent that will guide the next stage of work

Define / Plan does not decide *how* a solution will be delivered. It determines *what* matters enough to design for — and *why*.

The activities of this phase are outlined below and explored in more detail in the sections that follow.

Define/Plan Activities

The Define / Plan phase consists of the following activities, presented in the order they are typically applied.

10. **Empathy Mapping** deepens understanding of Experience Archetypes by making emotional, cognitive, and environmental pressures visible.
11. **Insight Synthesis** brings coherence to what has been observed, turning fragments of behaviour, contradiction, and constraint into shared meaning.
12. **Problem Statement Framing** names the problem worth solving — precisely, contextually, and without collapsing complexity too early.
13. **How Might We** reframes that problem into possibility, opening the solution space without committing to direction.
14. **Prioritisation Workshop** determines what moves forward into development, ensuring focus is intentional and defensible.

How Define Aligns With Plan in ITSM

In ITSM, Plan is where direction is set. Scope is agreed, priorities are established, and the organisation aligns on what work will move forward.

The Define phase in the HIT DDF™ serves the same moment — but with a different responsibility.

Define ensures the organisation is planning against the *right problem*.

Where Plan structures the work to be done, Define stabilises what that work is meant to address. It closes exploration, resolves competing interpretations, and establishes a clear problem frame before requirements, timelines, or delivery approaches are locked in.

Together:

- Define clarifies the problem
- Plan organises the response

Diamond One – Phase 2

This is the point where Diamond One concludes, with clarity strong enough to justify commitment.

Diamond One – Phase 2

Activity 10: Empathy Mapping

Making Lived Experience Visible

Empathy mapping is widely used in product and service design, particularly in consumer, digital, and market-led environments.

In those contexts, empathy maps are often used to:

- Explore unmet needs and motivations
- Test assumptions about customers or users
- Compare what a product offers against market expectations
- Inform feature prioritisation and value propositions

Questions commonly embedded in these canvases include:

- What does the market offer today?
- What alternatives exist?
- What frustrates users about current options?
- What would create differentiation or competitive advantage?

Empathy is the discipline of seeing the system from inside the work — understanding what information available, what pressures is are present, what trade-offs are being made, and what signals guide action in real time.

Used this way, empathy maps are frequently generative, they help teams imagine possibilities, identify opportunities, and explore what *could* be built.

How Humanising IT™ Uses Empathy Mapping Differently

Humanising IT™ adopts empathy mapping for a different purpose.

ITSM is not a market-driven product environment.

Services already exist. Systems are already live. Constraints are real and non-negotiable.

For this reason, empathy mapping in the HIT DDF™ is not used to explore market opportunity or customer desire.

Instead, it is used to:

- Stabilise understanding of lived experience
- Make operational reality visible
- Ensure the problem is defined from evidence, and empathy

Empathy maps in Humanising IT™ do **not** ask:

- What should we offer?
- What does the market expect?
- What would delight users?

They ask:

- What conditions are people operating under *right now*?
- What pressures are shaping behaviour?
- What signals guide action inside the system?
- What does it actually feel like to keep work moving here?

This is why empathy mapping appears after observation and synthesis, not before.

It is a convergent tool, not an ideation tool.

What an Empathy Map Captures

Empathy maps exist in many variations, but most follow a common structure. Typically, they organise experience around what people think and feel, see, say and do, and hear, sometimes supplemented with pains and gains.

These canvases are widely available to download. The value lies not in the template itself, but in how evidence is selected, placed, and interpreted.

In Humanising IT™, the structure is used deliberately and conservatively, as a way of organising observed experience, not generating new insight or speculation.

Diamond One – Phase 2

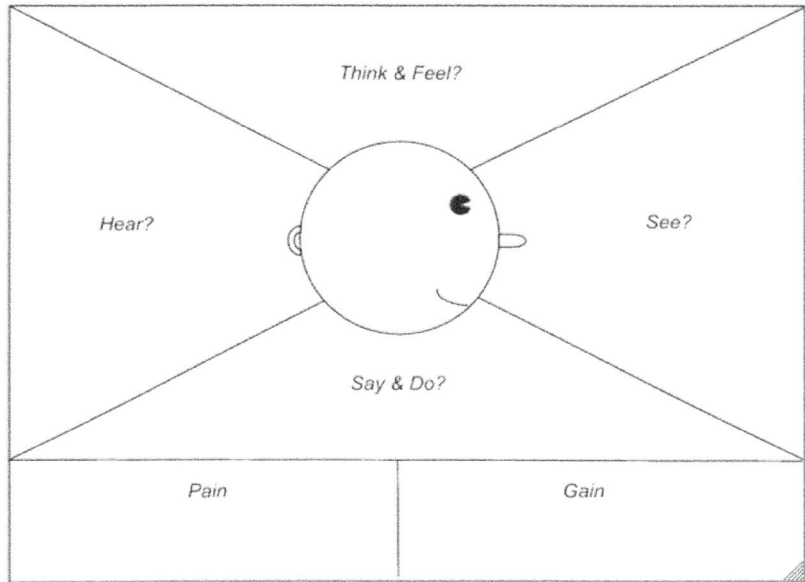

Figure 6: Empathy Map Canvas

What they say

Observable statements, questions, complaints, or silences that occur during interaction with the service.

What they think

Reasonable considerations or uncertainties shaped by the conditions they are operating under.

What they do

Observed actions in practice, including escalation, delay, workaround, avoidance, repetition, or compliance.

What they feel

Situational emotional responses triggered by interaction with the service, such as frustration, anxiety, relief, confidence, or resignation.

Some teams also note Pains (effort, friction, risk) and Gains (progress, clarity, reassurance) when these reflect patterns already evidenced.

Example: Empathy Mapping the Escalator Archetype

To illustrate how empathy mapping is used in practice, consider the *Escalator* Experience Archetype.

Based on evidence gathered during Service Safari and Experience Flow Sketching, the empathy map begins to take shape:

What they say
- "I've already tried logging this — it's not moving."
- "I need someone senior to look at this."

What they think
- "If I don't escalate this now, it will stall."
- "Following the standard path will cost me time I don't have."

What they do
- Bypass formal escalation routes
- Contact senior stakeholders directly
- Reopen or duplicate tickets to regain visibility

What they feel
- Urgency
- Frustration
- Relief once attention is secured

Seen together, these elements do not describe a difficult individual. They describe a rational response to conditions where progress feels opaque and delay carries risk.

The empathy map does not explain *why* escalation occurs , that work is done later.

> It simply makes visible what it is like to operate inside the system from this position.

How the Activity Is Conducted

Empathy Mapping is a convergent activity. It consolidates what has already been observed across Diamond One into a single, structured view of experience.

The team selects one Experience Archetype at a time and works only with existing evidence: observations from Service Safari, signals from Desktop Research, behavioural patterns already identified, and insights surfaced through Experience Flow Sketching and the Design vs Reality Review.

Using the canvas, evidence is organised into the four dimensions. The rule is explicit: if it was not observed, it does not belong. Entries are routinely challenged by asking where the evidence came from and whether it reflects something seen or heard, rather than inferred.

Once complete, the map is reviewed as a whole to reveal the conditions shaping behaviour, the pressures being absorbed, and the signals guiding response. This creates a stable, shared understanding of experience that feeds directly into the next HIT DDF™ activity: **Insight Synthesis**.

Activity 11: Proto personas

What personas are — and why they exist in design

In design practice, **personas** are detailed representations of groups of people who are expected to use a product, service, or system.

They are typically based on:
- Research across multiple users
- Observed behaviours and needs
- Goals, constraints, and motivations
- Patterns validated over time

Personas are used to support **design decision-making**.
They help teams answer questions such as:
- Who are we designing for when priorities conflict?
- Whose needs should take precedence?
- How will different groups experience this change?

In mature design environments, personas are treated as a craft.
Creating them well requires:
- Specialist skills
- Rigorous research
- Time, access, and budget
- Careful validation

Done properly, personas become powerful tools for guiding design choices.

Why Humanising IT™ does not create full personas

Most IT organisations are **not design studios**.
They are operating environments with:

- Live services
- Real risk
- Limited time
- Constrained access to users
- Accountability for stability and continuity

While personas are valuable, creating them properly is **beyond the capability, remit, and resourcing of most IT departments** — and attempting to do so often results in shallow or fictional outputs that undermine trust.

Humanising IT™ **respects the craft of design.**

Rather than performing it poorly, the HIT DDF™ deliberately avoids full persona creation.

Instead, the framework focuses first on:

- Understanding perception (RIPP)
- Surfacing assumptions
- Identifying behavioural patterns (Experience Archetypes)
- Grounding insight in real operational evidence

Only once that understanding is in place does Humanising IT™ introduce **proto personas**.

Diamond One – Phase 2

Figure 7: Persona (Design Practice Example)

Personas like this require deep research, specialist skills, and sustained access to users.

In most IT service management environments, this level of research is neither feasible nor appropriate, particularly when services are already live and under operational pressure.

Diamond One – Phase 2

HIT DDF™ Proto Persona Canvas

Provisional | Evidence-Informed | Human-Centred

 HIT DDF™

Humanising IT™

Proto Persona Title
(Describe the context, not the individual)

1. Context & Accountability
What is this person acountable for in practice?

2. Operating Conditions
What conditions shape how they experience the service?

3. What Matters Most
What do they need from the service to do their job well?

4. Typical Experience with the Service
What is it like to interact with the service today?

5. Typical Experience with the Service
What is it like to interact with the service today?

6. Observed Responses *(Experience Archetypes)*
Which Experience Archetypes may appear for this proto persona?
☐ (Select all that apply)
☐
☐
☐

7. Pressures Shaping Perspective
What pressures influence how this person interprets and responds to the *situation*?

8. Status
☐ Provisional
☐ Evidence-informed
☐ Not a validated persona

Notes:

8. What This Proto Persona Is Used For
How will this proto persona support decision-making?

Reminder
☐ Proto personas are working profiles based on current understanding. They may evolve *as insight deepens* or be replaced by deeper design work.

Proto persona used in Humanising IT™ to support alignment and decision-making without over-claiming certainty.

What a proto persona is

Proto personas are **simple, provisional profiles** that help teams align on *who is being affected* by the current system, based on what is known at that point in time.

They are:

- Grounded in evidence gathered through the HIT DDF™
- Informed by Experience Archetypes and Empathy Mapping
- Intentionally lightweight and non-exhaustive

Proto personas are **not validated personas.**
They are working representations used to support:

- Problem framing
- Prioritisation
- Alignment between IT and the business
- Handover into design or change conversations

They make insight **usable**, without over-claiming accuracy.

How proto personas are used in practice

A proto persona might describe:

- The context a person is operating within
- The pressures they are under
- What they are accountable for
- How they typically experience the service

Importantly, a single proto persona may exhibit **multiple Experience Archetypes**, depending on conditions.

Proto personas are used to:
- Clarify who a problem is impacting most
- Avoid designing for "everyone"
- Keep discussions grounded in lived experience
- Support decision-making without pretending certainty

They may evolve as understanding deepens, or be replaced entirely if deeper design work follows.

Experience Archetypes and Personas

Understanding the Difference

In Humanising IT™, **Experience Archetypes** and **personas** are often mentioned together, but they are not the same thing and are not used for the same purpose.

A **persona** represents a type of person.

It is used in design to describe a group of users with shared characteristics, goals, needs, and constraints. Personas help teams keep real people in mind when making design decisions, particularly when choosing between different design options.

An **Experience Archetype**, on the other hand, represents a pattern of behaviour.

It describes how people tend to act when interacting with a service under certain conditions, such as time pressure, risk, lack of visibility, or operational stress.

The key distinction is this:

Personas describe people

Experience Archetypes describe behaviour

These two concepts operate at different levels.

A single persona can exhibit multiple Experience Archetypes, depending on the situation. For example, the same person may follow the process calmly in one context, escalate quickly in another, and create workarounds when under sustained pressure. The behaviour changes — the person does not.

This distinction is critical in ITSM. Many problems are incorrectly framed as issues with "users" or "roles", when in reality they are the result of conditions created by systems, **processes, and constraints**. Experience Archetypes allow teams to examine those behavioural patterns without labelling or stereotyping people.

In Humanising IT™, Experience Archetypes are used first to understand what is happening and why. Personas (or proto personas) are only introduced later, once behavioural patterns are understood and the focus shifts toward framing problems and informing decisions.

By keeping archetypes and personas distinct, Humanising IT™ avoids oversimplification and ensures that behaviour is examined in context, not attributed to personality or job title.

Activity 12: Insight Synthesis

Making Sense of What Has Been Found

By the time teams reach Insight Synthesis, a large amount of evidence has been gathered. This includes documented system intent, operational data, and patterns in how people adapt in practice.

> *What exists at this point is not a lack of information, but an excess of it.*

Insight Synthesis is the activity that brings these **separate pieces of evidence** together and asks what they mean *in relation to one another*. It is where teams stop collecting and *sense-making* — stepping back to look across what has already been surfaced so that individual observations are no longer treated as isolated issues, but recognised as part of a system dynamic that continues to shape behaviour.

Finding vs Insight

It is worth pausing here to clarify the distinction between a *finding* and an *insight*.

A finding is something you observed.

It is a piece of evidence a behaviour, a quote, a pattern, a signal, a gap between design and reality.

Synthesis is the act of working across multiple findings. It involves grouping, comparing, and examining evidence to understand what connects it, what repeats, and what conditions appear to shape behaviour *(often referred to as affinity mapping)*.

An insight is what that finding means.

It is not a restatement of what was seen, but an explanation of what those findings reveal about how the system works.

A Simple Example Outside of IT

Findings:

- Customers frequently ask staff how long their order will take, even when a queue display is visible.

- The display updates only at fixed intervals, not in real time.
- Staff often reassure customers verbally, even when the system is functioning as designed.

Insight:
Customers do not trust static progress indicators. They seek human confirmation when waiting carries uncertainty, because reassurance matters more than technical accuracy in moments of delay.

A Simple Example Inside of IT

Findings:

- During Service Safari, several people checked three different systems to confirm the same piece of information.
- Desktop Research showed the documented process stated that "the system of record is always up to date."
- Experience Archetypes revealed repeated patterns of double-checking before action.
- In conversation, people described the data as "mostly right, but not reliable enough."

Insight:

People do not fully trust the system of record. They verify information across multiple sources because the perceived risk of acting on inaccurate data is higher than the effort required to recheck it.

Why Synthesis Is Necessary

> *In ITSM, momentum often pushes teams to act as soon as something is visible or measurable.*

Insight Synthesis deliberately slows that impulse. It creates a pause where the organisation asks not what should we fix, but what is the system consistently producing and why.

By the time teams reach Insight Synthesis, they already *know a lot.*

They know how the service is meant to work.

They know how it actually works.

They have evidence of behaviour, adaptation, workarounds, pressure points, and mismatch.

What they don't yet have is a shared understanding of *what it all adds up to.*

Without this shared understanding, this is how teams can end up responding to symptoms repeatedly — fixing tickets, tightening steps, adding controls — while the conditions producing those outcomes remain unchanged.

Insight Synthesis is necessary because **evidence on its own does not create meaning.**

These insights are provisional rather than final, but they are stable enough to support the next phase of work. They create the foundation for problem framing by ensuring that focus is earned through evidence, not assumed through opinion or urgency.

A Note on When Insights Emerge

In Humanising IT™, insight can emerge at any point during Discover / Strategy.
The Insight Synthesis activity does not initiate insight it consolidates it.

Activity 12: Problem Framing

Why This Will Feel Familiar — and Why It Is Different

IT professionals are no strangers to problem statements. They appear in incident reports, problem records, business cases, change proposals, and post-incident reviews. The format is familiar, and the discipline is well established.

Humanising IT™ does not challenge this discipline. What differs is not *how* a problem statement is written, but *when* it is written, and *what evidence informs it*.

In ITSM, problem statements are often created early because they serve an operational purpose. When something is failing, slowing work, or creating visible impact, the priority is stabilisation. A clearly articulated problem statement enables investigation, ownership, and coordinated action.

For example:

"Recurring incidents are being caused by failures in the authentication service."

This framing is entirely appropriate. It reflects the system view required to restore stability and manage risk.

Human-centred design introduces a different kind of problem work. It does not replace operational problem statements, nor does it invalidate them. Instead, it creates space *before commitment* to understand how a situation is being experienced, interpreted, and navigated by people within the system — particularly when issues persist, recur, or resist resolution.

At this point, the question is no longer whether IT has described a problem correctly, but whether the organisation has identified the right problem to solve before design and planning begin.

This book does not attempt to teach problem framing as a standalone discipline. Instead, it shows how problem framing functions within the HIT DDF™ — as the point where evidence from lived experience is translated into focus for planning and design.

Two Types of Problems — Two Different Moments

Not all problems serve the same purpose, and not all should be framed at the same time.

- **Operational problems** need to be framed early so instability can be contained and impact reduced.
- **Experience-based problems** need to be framed later, once the conditions shaping behaviour are visible.

Human-centred design uses problem framing to articulate lived experience *before* deciding what should change. The aim is not speed, but accuracy, ensuring effort is directed at the conditions that sustain the issue, not just the symptoms that surface it.

Humanising IT™ applies this discipline to IT services, focusing on how constraints, pressure, and system dynamics shape behaviour in real operating conditions.

What Problem Framing Enables

Because it is grounded in evidence, a Humanising IT™ problem statement carries less judgement, creates less defensiveness, and invites inquiry rather than blame. It does not close the conversation. It opens the right one, providing a stable foundation for planning, prioritisation, and design in the next phase.

If the statement generates curiosity and nods of recognition, it's right.

If it generates defensiveness, it needs refinement.

It should explain **why the situation keeps happening**, not just what is happening.

This becomes the foundation for **How Might We** and the rest of the Define / Plan phase.

Activity 14: How Might We

Opening Opportunity Without Committing Too Early

How Might We (HMW) questions are used to open opportunity.

In human-centred design, they create a controlled pause between understanding a problem and deciding what to do about it. That pause matters. It prevents teams from collapsing straight into familiar fixes, preferred tools, or pre-approved solutions.

Humanising IT™ adopts this same technique and applies it to ITSM — where behaviour is shaped by constraints, pressure, and system dynamics rather than choice alone.

At this point in the HIT DDF™, the problem has already been framed clearly. HMW does not redefine the problem. It holds it open.

> *What HMW does especially well is surface multiple directions for change without forcing selection. It turns a single, well-understood problem into a set of opportunity areas the organisation could explore before committing time, money, or authority.*

In practice, this means:

- The team stays anchored to the evidence gathered so far
- Possibility is explored without abandoning rigour
- Solutions are not chosen prematurely
- Opportunity is expanded before it is narrowed

HMW marks the transition from *understanding what is happening* to *exploring what could change*, without losing sight of why the situation exists in the first place.

The Theory Behind How Might We

How Might We questions are deliberately structured to do three things at once:

1. **Keep the problem open**

"**How**" signals that the answer is not yet known.

It prevents premature closure and resists the instinct to defend a single interpretation or solution.

2. Anchor exploration to a real constraint

"**Might**" introduces possibility *within limits.*

It acknowledges that constraints exist — technical, organisational, human — while still allowing exploration.

3. Preserve shared ownership of the question

"**We**" signals that the problem is systemic, not personal.

It removes blame and reframes the challenge as something the system must respond to collectively.

This structure is intentional.

Each word plays a role in keeping inquiry alive without drifting into abstraction.

Bridging Into Diamond Two

Working Example

As we close out Diamond One, two activities become especially important: **Problem Framing** and **How Might We**. Together, they create the bridge between understanding the problem and exploring what might be possible next.

- Problem Framing gives us a clear, evidence-based view of the tension between how the system is designed and how people actually need to operate.
- How Might We holds that clarity open just long enough to explore possibility and opportunity without collapsing into premature solutions.

To see how these two activities work in practice, we now turn to **Experience Archetypes** — the patterns that reveal how people adapt when systems do not fully match the realities of their work.

Typical ITSM Problem Statement

"The CMDB is inaccurate."

Humanising IT™ Problem Framing

Teams struggle to maintain accurate configuration data because the effort feels high, the value feels low, and the system doesn't reflect how work actually happens.

This reframing shifts the focus from "the CMDB is broken" to the **human and system conditions** that make accuracy difficult.

Relevant Experience Archetypes

- **The Workaround Artist**

  People bypass the CMDB because it slows them down or doesn't reflect real work.

- **The Silent Sufferer**

  People don't report inaccuracies because it feels pointless or risky.

- **The Process Guardian**

  Individuals become the human buffer, manually enforcing accuracy the system can't sustain.

These archetypes reveal the behavioural tensions that sit underneath CMDB failure.

How Might We Questions

- How might we reduce the effort required to keep configuration data accurate?
- How might we make the value of accurate data visible and meaningful to the people who maintain it?
- How might we align configuration practices with how work actually happens?
- How might we design a CMDB experience that people trust and want to use?

These questions open up the opportunity space without collapsing into solutions.

Opportunity Areas

The HMWs surface several opportunity areas, the thematic directions the organisation could explore:

- **Reducing the manual effort required to maintain configuration data**
- **Improving the usability and experience of updating the CMDB**
- **Aligning CMDB processes with real workflows and incentives**
- **Increasing visibility of the value and impact of accurate data**
- **Improving supplier participation and integration pathways**

These are not solutions.

They are the different moves the organisation could make in response to the reframed problem.

And these are exactly what DVF will evaluate next.

Diamond One – Phase 2

Introducing DVF: Want, Should, Can

Before moving into the Prioritisation Workshop, the final activity in the HIT DDF™, it's worth pausing to look at the input that helps stakeholders decide **which opportunity will be taken into Diamond Two**.

That decision is the major output of Diamond One.

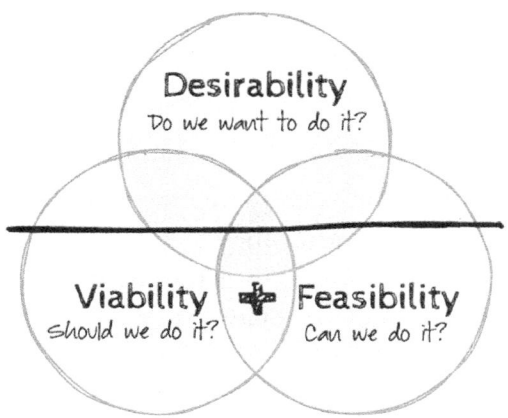

Figure 8: DVF Model

Humanising IT™ uses the DVF model to guide this choice. The model helps the group prioritise based on:

- **Desirability** — Does this matter to the people who experience the system?
- **Viability** — Does this align with how the organisation actually behaves?
- **Feasibility** — Can we realistically deliver and sustain this?

The DVF Model: A Lens for Deciding What Moves Forward

Once the design team has surfaced the problem framing and the How Might We questions, the next step is to decide **which opportunity** will move into Diamond Two.

Because as the saying goes: ***you cannot do everything***.

DVF gives teams a structured way to evaluate ideas before committing time, energy, and investment.

It isn't a scoring tool or a governance mechanism — it's a lens that ensures ideas are examined from the perspectives that matter in human systems.

DVF is not part of classic HCD.

In HCD, it is sometimes used informally after ideation to help choose which ideas to prototype.

In Humanising IT™, DVF becomes a formal decision point at the end of Diamond One to select the opportunity that will enter Diamond Two.

Traditional ITSM decisions are often shaped by governance cycles, contracts, architecture, risk, or urgency.

DVF doesn't replace these forces — it **rebalances** them by adding the human, organisational, and capability lens that ITSM has historically underweighted.

Prioritising With DVF

DVF Applied to the CMDB

With the opportunity areas surfaced, the next step is to evaluate which one is worth taking into Diamond Two.

This is where the DVF model becomes essential.

We return to our earlier example.

The CMDB is a perfect illustration of why DVF matters.

On paper, the CMDB is desirable, viable, and feasible.

In practice, the lived experience tells a very different story.

The Experience Archetypes reveal why:

- **The Workaround Artist** bypasses the CMDB because it slows them down.
- **The Silent Sufferer** doesn't report inaccuracies because it feels pointless or risky.

- **The Process Guardian** becomes the human buffer, manually enforcing accuracy the system can't sustain.

These archetypes expose the human and organisational tensions that DVF is designed to surface *before* investment.

Desirability — Does This Matter to People?

Desirability asks whether the opportunity is meaningful for the people who will live with it.

For the CMDB, the key questions include:

- Do frontline teams want a simpler way to maintain configuration data?
- Do they see value in accurate configuration information?
- Does the current CMDB experience feel intuitive or painful?
- Do people trust the data enough to use it?
- Would improving the CMDB make their day-to-day work easier?
- Does this reduce frustration, rework, or escalation risk?

Insight:

Frontline teams often see CMDB updates as "extra admin" with no visible benefit — low desirability.

This is exactly what the Workaround Expert and Silent Sufferer archetypes reveal.

Viability — Does This Fit How the Organisation Really Works?

Viability tests whether the opportunity aligns with the organisation's actual behaviour, culture, incentives, and pace — not the idealised version.

For the CMDB, viability questions include:

- Do teams have the bandwidth to maintain configuration data?
- Does the rate of change in the environment make accuracy unrealistic?
- Are ownership and accountability clear?

- Do incentives support accuracy, or speed?
- Do suppliers operate in ways that align with CMDB expectations?
- Does the organisation tolerate ambiguity, or require precision?

Insight:

If the environment changes daily and ownership is unclear, the CMDB may be theoretically viable but practically unviable.

This is the world the Process Guardian lives in every day.

Feasibility — Can We Deliver and Sustain This?

Feasibility examines capability, integration pathways, data conditions, supplier participation, and operating model maturity.

For the CMDB, feasibility questions include:

- Do we have the capability to integrate discovery tools effectively?
- Can suppliers reliably update data?
- Do we have the governance maturity to maintain accuracy?
- Are the data models realistic for our environment?
- Can we sustain the discipline required?
- Do we have the technical pathways to automate updates?

Insight:

Many organisations lack the integration maturity to automate updates — feasibility risk.

This is where the Process Guardian becomes the fallback mechanism, often for years.

Putting It All Together via the DVF

The CMDB example shows why initiatives fail not because the idea is wrong, but because:

- It's not desirable to the people who maintain it

- It's not viable in the real organisational environment
- It's not feasible given capability and maturity

DVF makes these truths visible before investment — while change is still cheap.

The result is a shortlist the organisation can commit to with confidence — setting up the next step:

The business and IT handshake, where both sides align on what will move into Diamond Two.

Activity 15: Prioritisation Workshop

In traditional ITSM, prioritisation often occurs implicitly.

Work is selected through a combination of urgency, authority, available budget, delivery convenience, or historical momentum. These forces are not inherently wrong. They are simply incomplete.

What Comes Into the Room

Before the Prioritisation Workshop begins, the team must be clear about **what is being brought into the room**. Prioritisation is only meaningful when it is grounded in evidence, not opinions or organisational politics. The workshop is therefore framed around a specific set of inputs that anchor the conversation in what the system has revealed so far.

The inputs include:

- **The Problem Statement** — a clear articulation of the problem the system is creating, not the solution anyone prefers.
- **Insight Synthesis** — the conditions, constraints, and behaviours that shape the current environment.
- **How Might We questions** — the structured prompts that open up a field of opportunities.
- **The DVF model** — the lens that ensures ideas are examined for desirability, viability, and feasibility before energy is committed.

These inputs form the boundary of the workshop. They prevent the conversation from collapsing into solution theatre or drifting into abstract debate. Everything that happens in the workshop is anchored to these artefacts.

Bringing Stakeholders Together

The Prioritisation Workshop brings together stakeholders from across the service environment — not just IT. This includes:

- Operational teams

- Business representatives
- Service owners
- Suppliers or partners (where relevant)
- Leaders accountable for outcomes
- People who live with the system every day

This mix is intentional.

IT alone cannot prioritise meaningfully because IT does not own the entire service boundary.

The workshop creates a shared space where different perspectives can see the same evidence at the same time.

The Handshake:

Where Business and IT Commit Together

Immediately after the Prioritisation Workshop and informed by DVF, comes a critical moment in the HIT DDF™ the handshake.

The handshake is not a sign-off.

It is a **mutual commitment**.

- The business commits to the problem that matters.
- IT commits to the opportunity that is feasible.
- Both commit to the path that is viable within the organisation's reality.

It is the moment where the organisation says:

"This is the opportunity we will pursue together."

Closing Out Diamond One

Diamond One ends with a shared understanding of the problem, the human and system conditions that shape it, and the opportunity most worth pursuing.

As outlined at the beginning of this book, the primary focus of this publication is **Diamond One**.

There is a reason for that.

This is where Humanising IT™ makes its most significant contribution. It brings the discipline, curiosity, and behavioural insight of human-centred design into a space that has historically prioritised process, tooling, and governance over lived experience.

But while this book focuses on Diamond One, the learning does not stop here.

ITSM can still benefit enormously from human-centred design principles in the later phases in how ideas are developed, tested, iterated, delivered and of course maintained.

Those phases have their own rhythms and practices, and they build on the clarity created in Diamond One.

Diamond Two is where the chosen opportunity is explored, shaped, and tested with the people who will live with the outcome.

This marks the end of Diamond One.

Now we turn to what happens when human-centred insight begins to reshape ITSM.

Chapter 6

Diamond Two – Phase 3

Develop/Design — Exploring Possibilities Before Anything Is Built

By the time designers reach Phase 3, a positive shift has occurred.

The Define/Plan phase has done its work: understanding is shared, focus is clear, and the organisation knows where attention is best directed.

Now comes a phase that feels familiar in name, but unfamiliar in practice.

Most IT professionals hear the word *develop* and instinctively think of building — coding, configuring, designing workflows, preparing releases. That association makes perfect sense: in the ITSM lifecycle, Build is where solutions take shape.

In the HIT DDF™, however, Develop means something different

But in the British Design Council's Double Diamond and in the HIT DDF™, **Develop is not about building yet.**

It is the phase *before* building.

It is the space where IT shapes possibilities rather than solutions.

Nothing here is coded.

Nothing is configured.

No vendor contract is signed.

This is not development work.

It is thinking work, structured, disciplined, low-risk exploration that protects the organisation from moving too quickly toward a single answer and heavy investment.

Develop/Design Activities

The activities and descriptions in the Develop/Design phase of the HIT DDF™ are outlined below. As noted earlier, this publication does not explore Diamond Two in depth; in this chapter, our focus is Ideation and Prototype Iteration / Refinement activities.

15. **Ideation:** A focused session to generate multiple ways the defined problem could be approached
16. **Low-Fidelity Prototyping:** Quick, disposable representations of ideas used to test assumptions early and cheaply.
17. **Co-Design and User Experience Testing:** Collaborative sessions where IT, business stakeholders, and users shape and test early concepts together to understand how people interpret, navigate, and respond to emerging ideas.
18. **Iteration and Refinement:** Improving early prototypes based on what testing reveals to reduce uncertainty.
19. **Opportunity Alignment Workshop:** A checkpoint to confirm the emerging direction before moving toward higher-fidelity design.

How Develop Aligns With Design in ITSM

In traditional ITSM, *Design* is the stage where teams shape how a service or change will work before anything is built or released. It is the space where options are explored, risks are surfaced, and the organisation decides what the future service experience should look like.

The Develop phase in the HIT DDF™ aligns directly with this intent but expands it.

Where ITSM Design focuses on defining the service components, Humanising IT™ Develop/Design focuses on understanding how people will interpret, use, and experience those components in the real environment. It brings the human lens forward, ensuring design decisions are grounded in how people actually work, not just how technology or process models expect them to work.

Both phases share the same purpose:
- Explore options before committing
- Understand constraints early
- Reduce risk before build
- Shape the direction of the solution

ITSM Design defines the service.
HIT DDF™ Develop tests how the service will behave in practice.

By aligning these two perspectives, IT gains a more complete view — not only how a service should work in theory, but how it will behave when real people interact with it in real conditions, long before significant investment is committed.

A Simpler Way to Think About Develop
It's important to be clear about something:
IT already evaluates options today.
Architects consider multiple paths.
Project teams compare approaches.
Design authorities weigh alternatives.

What the Develop phase adds is **the human lens** — a way of exploring solution directions that reflects everything surfaced in Discover and Define, real environments, constraints, behaviours, pressures, and moments that matter.

Build, in the ITSM sense, sits later, in the **Deliver** phase, when IT begins preparing something for operational reality:

Develop Is Divergent — But Structured
Like Discover, in diamond 1, Develop is a divergent phase.
But the two are different:
- **Discover widens understanding of the problem.**

- **Develop widens the possibilities for solving it.**

Both require curiosity.

Develop requires discipline to stay anchored to the defined problem.

Develop does not open the organisation to wild creativity.

It expands thinking inside the constraints surfaced in Define:

Activity 16: Ideation

Expanding the Space of What's Possible

As the name suggests, ideation is about ideas. It is a well-established technique in human-centred design and one that Humanising IT™ encourages within ITSM. Ideation is the point where a team generates many different ways a problem could be solved.

> *By expanding the field of options before narrowing it, ideation ensures that the solutions considered later in the process are grounded in possibility, not familiarity.*

In simple terms, ideation says:
"We understand the problem. Now let's explore all the possible ways we could approach it."

Because this is a divergent stage, the goal is **quantity, not quality**. The task is to open up the space of possibility, not to narrow it prematurely. To do this well, teams temporarily suspend the constraints that normally shape IT decision-making.

During ideation, teams are encouraged to:
- Forget bias
- Forget best practice
- Forget why something "won't work"
- Forget constraints for a moment
- Imagine no budget limits
- Imagine unlimited resources
- Imagine no technical debt
- Imagine no legacy constraints
- Imagine every option is possible
- Imagine starting fresh with a blank page

The point is not to pretend these conditions are real. The point is to free the team from habitual patterns of thinking so new possibilities can surface, possibilities that rarely emerge in day-to-day operational environments.

Ideation helps teams avoid jumping to the first solution, or the safest, least expensive, and most familiar one. Instead, teams explore the full range of what *could* work.

Common ideation techniques include sketching flows, listing alternatives, imagining different service models, quick role plays, or simply asking, **"What else could work here?"**

A Simple Example Outside of IT

Coffee Cup

To make ideation concrete, let's look at a simple, everyday example outside of IT.

Imagine a design team tasked with improving the design of a reusable coffee cup. Before anything is built or tested, the team begins with ideation.

The goal isn't to decide.

The goal is to **create options**.

In a short session, the team produces ideas such as:

- A collapsible cup that folds flat
- A cup with a built-in temperature gauge
- A magnetic lid that snaps shut automatically
- A cup that changes colour when the drink is too hot
- A removable inner liner for easy cleaning
- A biodegradable version

Some ideas are practical.
Some are unrealistic.
Some are playful or strange.
And that's exactly the point.
Ideation expands the solution space before anyone narrows it.

A Simple Example Inside IT:

CMDB

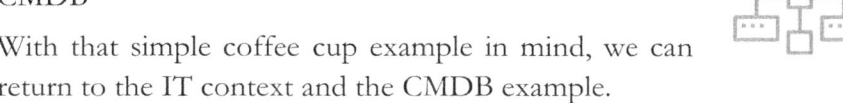

With that simple coffee cup example in mind, we can return to the IT context and the CMDB example.
During the CMDB ideation session, the team applied the same principles:
No constraints, no feasibility filter, no judgement

This produced ideas such as:

- Letting the CMDB expire CIs automatically unless someone renews them
- Using AR glasses so updates happen based on what engineers look at
- Running the CMDB like a stock market, where CIs gain or lose "value"
- Making the CMDB read-only for a week to see what people actually rely on
- Letting AI delete 50% of the CMDB overnight to test what truly matters

These ideas weren't intended to be implemented.
They were intended to **stretch thinking**, expose assumptions, and reveal what people actually value.

Why Ideas Matter

(Even If None Are Used)

Ideas like these:

- Expose assumptions
- Reveal what people actually value
- Show where the pain really is
- Spark more practical versions
- Challenge the "we can't do that" mindset

- Widen the solution space far beyond usual ITSM thinking

And crucially:

You don't need to implement the crazy idea, you need the insight it unlocks.

Once a team has generated a wide range of possibilities through ideation, the next step is to **test those possibilities quickly and cheaply** *before committing to any direction.*
This is where prototyping begins.

Activity 17: Iteration and Refinement

Learn First, Commit Later

Once a team has generated a wide range of possibilities through ideation, the next step is to **test those possibilities quickly and cheaply** before committing to any direction. This is where prototyping begins.

> *A prototype might be a sketch, a role-play, a simulated conversation, or a short operational trial.*

> *What matters is not the fidelity, it is the learning.*

In most IT environments, "testing" usually begins with a Proof of Concept or a Pilot. These are familiar rituals: structured, governed, often vendor-supported, and typically initiated only after the organisation has already chosen a direction, justified a business case, and aligned stakeholders. By that point, **the organisation is no longer exploring the idea it is validating it**

The space for discovery has already closed.

Using the principles of human-centred design, Humanising IT™ brings testing forward much earlier by introducing prototyping as a fast, low-risk way to explore how ideas behave in the real environment.

What a Prototype Really Is and What is Not

A prototype is the **smallest, simplest, quickest** way to test the **riskiest assumption** behind an idea.

It is **not** a technical build.
It is **not** a partial configuration.
It is **not** a mini-project or early release.

A prototype exists for one purpose only:

To find out whether the idea behaves the way we expect, before anyone spends time, money, or credibility committing to it.

Prototyping helps IT answer questions that technical tests cannot.

Prototyping lets IT see that early, cheaply, and honestly.

Prototypes are meant to be thrown away.
They validate thinking, not technology.

A Simple Example Outside IT

Prototyping a New Coffee Cup

To make prototyping tangible, let's return to the reusable coffee cup example — but this time, after ideation has produced many possibilities.

The design team selects a few ideas to explore and creates very rough prototypes:

- A paper model to test size
- A clay model to test grip
- A plastic shell to test lid shape
- A cardboard sleeve to test heat protection

None of these hold liquid.
None function as a real cup.

But they allow the team to **learn fast**.

What the prototype reveals

When people interact with the mock-ups, the team discovers:

- The cup is too wide to hold comfortably
- The lid is difficult to open with one hand
- The heat sleeve slips when the cup tilts
- The "spill-proof" lip drips when people walk

These insights would never appear in a meeting or a requirements document.

They only emerge when someone tries something, even if it's rough.

A Simple Example Inside IT

In the CMDB example, the team used prototyping long before touching tooling or configuration. They ran small, fast tests such as:

- Walking through short incident scenarios to identify which CMDB information people rely on under pressure
- Role-playing a CI creation conversation to see where interpretation diverged
- Testing whether teams could operate for a day using only a "minimum viable CMDB" dataset
- Trialling a "renewal" concept where CIs expired unless someone confirmed they were still needed

Each prototype revealed how people interpret, navigate, and use CMDB information in the real environment insights no document or workshop could surface.

Prototyping in ITSM

IT already prototypes, just far too late in the lifecycle.

Examples include:

- Major incident simulations
- Dry runs before go-lives
- Walkthroughs of new workflows
- Tabletop continuity exercises

These are prototyping behaviours, but they occur when the direction is already chosen and changing course is expensive.

Humanising IT™ simply moves this behaviour earlier, when the stakes are low and the organisation can change its mind far more easily.

> As outlined earlier, this publication does not cover every activity in Diamond 2. We chose to focus on Ideation and Prototyping within Phase 3 because this is where ITSM can learn the most from human-centred design.
>
> Why this focus?
>
> ITSM does prototype, but we tend to do it only after the decision is made, the investment is committed, and changing course becomes costly, slow, or politically sensitive.
>
> Humanising IT™ brings this learning forward — to a point where the organisation can change its mind easily, cheaply, and without friction. This shift, from validating decisions late to exploring assumptions early, is one of the most powerful contributions human-centred design makes to ITSM practice.

Closing out Phase 3

By the end of Develop, the team has a **validated concept**: a clear direction shaped by insight, grounded in evidence, and aligned around a shared understanding of what the service must achieve. It defines the intent, the experience principles, and the assumptions that now need to be tested in the real environments where the service will live. What it does *not* produce is a working service — that is the work of Deliver.

The next chapter moves us into the Deliver / Build / Transition phase.
In Humanising IT™, this phase is still part of design, just as it is in Human-Centred Design.
But the reality that matters to ITSM, the reality of a live service, with all the complexity, variability, and skill required to run and maintain it, only appears later, in Maintain / Run.
That distinction matters.
Human-centred design ends at Deliver because its purpose is design.

Diamond Two – Phase 3

Run belongs to IT Operations, the strength of ITSM, and the place where the true behaviour of a service is ultimately revealed.

Chapter 7

Diamond Two – Phase 4

Deliver/Build/Transition - Making the Service Real

We have now reached a point where exploration has done its job.
The concept is clear enough, meaningful enough, and supported by enough evidence that it now needs to be tested in the environments where it will live.

This is the phase the Double Diamond calls Deliver and where Humanising IT™ aligns the Build / Transition phases of the ITSM lifecycle.

This phase is where the concept becomes usable. It's where experience testing, technical build, and organisational readiness come together so the service can succeed both technically and in everyday work.

Deliver/Build/Transition Activities

The activities in this phase focus on refining the experience, building what matters, and preparing people and operations.

As with the Develop/Design phase, this publication does not explore every activity in depth.
Those will be addressed in future publications.

In this book, we focus on Activity 20, as this activity is central to the Humanising IT™ framework. All activities of the Deliver/Build/Transition phase are outlined below:

20. Experience Validation ad Refinement

Bringing the concept into real-world conditions to see how it behaves, then refining the experience and workflow in response to what surfaces.

21. **Technical Build #**
Creating, configuring, and integrating the technical components needed to support the validated experience.

22. **System-Level Testing and Validation**
Ensuring the service works end-to-end — technically, functionally, and in the environments where it will operate.

23. **Release Readiness**
Bringing together role clarity, team readiness, operational alignment, and release planning so the service can enter real-world use with stability, confidence, and minimal disruption.

How Deliver Aligns with Build/Transition in ITSM

Traditional ITSM describes two phases after design:

- **Build** — creating, configuring, and testing the solution
- **Transition** — preparing the solution for release, adoption, and operation

In the HIT DDF™, these phases sit together inside Deliver. Not because they are replaced, but because bringing them together creates a smoother, more connected path from concept to real-world use.

Deliver strengthens Build and Transition by ensuring that:

- The build is shaped by real experience
- The transition is grounded in how people actually work
- The service is prepared for both technical and human success

> *Humanising IT™ is* **not** *asking IT teams to become organisational change managers, nor is it redefining OCM as part of IT's scope. Many organisations already have strong OCM capabilities, and the HIT DDF™ works alongside them, not instead of them.*
>
> *The HIT DDF™ ensures OCM has the* **right insights** *at the* **right time** *to support adoption.*

Together, these elements make Deliver the place where Build and Transition come together in a more integrated, experience-led way. It ensures the service moves from concept to real-world use with clarity, alignment, and the right level of readiness for both people and operations.

Deliver Is Convergent — But Practically Grounded

Deliver is a convergent phase, but not in the abstract, narrowing-ideas sense.

It is convergent in the **practical, operational, real-world** sense: this is where the concept is tested against the conditions it must survive.

Where Develop expands possibilities for how the experience could work, Deliver narrows the solution into something that can actually operate — technically, behaviourally, and organisationally.

It asks:

- Does the experience hold up under real conditions?
- Does the build support the experience people actually need?
- Can teams use it without workarounds?
- Can operations sustain it without friction?
- Does the service behave the way the concept promised?

Deliver is disciplined, grounded, and unforgiving in the best possible way: **anything that doesn't work here will not work in production.**

Clarifying the Difference Between Develop and Deliver

It's important to restate the distinction between **Develop** and **Deliver**, because both involve testing, but they test different things for different purposes.

Develop tests the concept. Deliver tests the service.

Develop explores whether the idea works as an experience:
How people move through it, what they notice, what they need, and where the flow makes sense or falls away.

Deliver explores whether the service works in real conditions:
Whether the build supports the experience, whether teams can use it, and whether operations can sustain it.

And in our experience, these two forms of testing are not typically separated — or even explicitly recognised, in traditional ITSM practice.

A Simple Example Outside IT

The Coffee Cup

In the coffee-cup conversation, we used a simple analogy:

- **Develop is where you watch someone hold a rough prototype of the cup** — a cardboard cut-out, a clay shape, a paper mock-up, anything quick and disposable that lets you see how they naturally grip, tilt, and use it.

- **Deliver is where you make the cup** — shaping the handle, adjusting the weight, choosing the material, and ensuring it survives real-world use.

The insight is straightforward:

You don't design the handle until you understand how people actually hold the cup.

Develop gives you that understanding.
Deliver turns that understanding into something people can use in practice.

A Simple Example Inside IT

The CMDB is one of the clearest places where the difference between Develop and Deliver becomes essential.

Most organisations jump straight into building the CMDB — defining classes, attributes, relationships, and data sources, without first understanding how people actually use configuration information.

> *This is the equivalent of designing the coffee-cup handle before watching how anyone holds the cup*

Humanising IT™ separates these two steps so the CMDB becomes something people can use in real work, not just something that looks complete on paper.

Activity:21: Prototype Testing & Experience Refinement

Bringing the concept into real-world conditions and refining it based on how people actually live it

Within the HIT DDF™, Prototype Testing & Experience Refinement exists because **Deliver is not a traditional IT handover.**

Most IT professionals know the familiar moment: The project is "done," documents are complete, the checklist is green, and the handover conversation begins. Everything looks right on paper — so surely everything will work in practice.

> *Traditional handovers were never designed to answer these questions. They focused on **information transfer**, not **experience ownership**.*

This is where the disconnect lives.

ITSM frameworks have evolved. ITIL™, Agile, DevOps, Lean, and SRE have all pushed IT toward faster delivery, better flow, and tighter feedback loops. The movement is absolutely heading in the right direction.

Yet even with all that progress, the **experience gap** remains.

We still face the same unanswered questions:

- Who owns the experience of Incident Management — not the process, the experience?
- Who decides whether these experiences work for the humans who rely on them every day?
- Who ensures the service makes sense under pressure, not just in documentation?

Deliver changes that.

By the time a service reaches this phase, IT and the business have already walked through the lived experience together — the pressure, the ambiguity, the moments that matter, the behavioural demands, the handoffs, and the environmental realities.

The handover is no longer:
"Here's the process. Operations will take it from here."
It becomes:
"We've tested this together.

We've seen where it works, where it strains, and how people will actually live it."

It closes the ownership gap.
And it begins to answer the question ITSM has never fully solved:
Who owns the experience?
Deliver ensures the answer is no longer "no one."

What Prototype Testing & Experience Refinement Actually Does
This activity takes the validated concept from Develop and exposes it to **real operational conditions**.
It is not a demonstration.
It is not a walkthrough.
It is a **stress test of the lived experience**, using the same pressures, constraints, and system noise that teams face every day.

This requires:

- Real data, with all its gaps, inconsistencies, and edge cases
- Real roles, performing their actual responsibilities, not acting out scripts
- Real operational contexts, including time pressure, handoffs, escalations, and competing priorities
- Real systems, with their quirks, delays, and integration behaviours

Prototype Testing & Experience Refinement reveals:

- Where the experience collapses under load
- Where people hesitate, backtrack, or create workarounds

- Where information is missing, misleading, or overwhelming
- Where the workflow needs reinforcement, simplification, or redesign
- Where the concept genuinely supports decision-making under pressure

This is the moment where the service is tested as a **lived experience**, it is where early thinking meets operational reality and only the parts that survive move forward.

The Business–IT Handshake

A Different Kind of Approval

Deliver creates a different kind of alignment between IT and the business.
Not a formal sign-off. Not a document review. Not a steering-committee approval.

By the time a service reaches this phase, both sides have already:

- Defined the problem together
- Shaped the insights together
- Selected the concept together
- Tested the experience together

The "handshake" here is simple: **Both sides understand how the service is meant to work in practice.**

This is not business approval of an IT-designed solution.
It is a shared operational understanding built through the earlier phases of the HIT DDF™.

> *"We built this together.*
> *And we will Run and Maintain it together."*

When build begins, the business is not validating something unfamiliar. They are supporting the creation of something they already recognise, understand, and expect to work.

Deliver is where this becomes visible — where the partnership formed in Discover, Define, and Develop becomes a **shared commitment to operation**:

Closing Out Phase 4

Deliver/Build/Transition is the point where intent becomes operation. It is where the concept is tested under the conditions it must survive, where the build is shaped by lived experience, and where the transition is grounded in how people actually work. By the end of this phase, the service is no longer an idea or a design artefact. It is something real, usable, and ready to enter the environments it was created for.

With Deliver, the experience gap that has long separated IT and the business begins to close. Both sides now share a practical understanding of how the service behaves, what it demands, and what it enables. This is the foundation that allows the service to move into real-world use with clarity, confidence, and importantly, shared ownership

Diamond Two – Phase 4

Before we move into what we believe is the most important part of any service, IT Operations, let's be clear about what "running and maintaining a service" actually means.

Chapter 8

Maintain & Run

What "Running and Maintaining a Service" Really Means

And Why It Shapes Experience More Than Design

You may have heard the phrase "keeping the lights on" often said both affectionately and dismissively, as if running IT operations were as simple as flicking a switch. It's meant to describe the reality of IT ops. It doesn't even come close.

"Keeping the lights on" dramatically undersells what running a service requires.

Running a service means:

- Absorbing variability that was never documented or predicted
- Responding to demand that refuses to behave as forecasts suggest
- Living with vendor contracts written years ago by people no longer in the organisation
- Carrying technical debt you didn't choose and can't immediately fix
- Operating processes shaped by system constraints rather than human reality

And it means navigating the emotional landscape of users who arrive frustrated, anxious, overwhelmed, or simply trying to do their job.

Running a service is where IT holds the weight of the organisation.
It is where trust must be rebuilt after every outage.
Where governance, risk, user perception, and operational truth collide.
Where multiple versions of reality must be held at once — the user's truth, the system's truth, the governance truth, the vendor truth.

In Maintain/Run, IT is at its most human.

And this is why Maintain/Run cannot remain outside the design conversation.

This phase of the ITSM lifecycle shapes the lived experience far more than any document, workshop, or approval ever could.

Where Experience Lives

Most design disciplines naturally conclude at delivery.

A product ships.
A service launches.
A feature goes live.

In human-centred design, the Double Diamond ends when the solution reaches the user. Not because designers believe their work is "done," but because the discipline was created for project-based environments where delivery is the finish line.

IT is different.

Delivery is not the end, it is the beginning.

The moment something goes live, two realities collide:

1. **Human behaviour in real environments**, and
2. **The ITSM ecosystem that must run, support, and sustain it**

Traditional human-centred design stops at handover because that is where its scope ends.
IT services, however, *start* their real life at that point.
This is why the HIT DDF™ extends beyond the Double-Diamond.
It connects design to the operational world.

Human-centred design is a design practice.

HIT DDF™ adds the operational dimension it was never required to carry.

Alignment To All ITSM Frameworks

In this phase of the HIT DDF™, we do not prescribe a specific framework or operating model. IT organisations already work within structures such as ITIL, DevOps, SRE, COBIT, or internally defined models, and the HIT DDF™ is designed to sit alongside these, not replace them.

What matters is this: **Every technique used throughout this book can be applied directly to IT operations, processes, and systems.**

The same tools that help you understand users, surface friction, map behaviours, and design improvements in both diamonds are equally powerful in Maintain/Run phase.

For example, the same approaches we explored you would use to improve a customer-facing journey can be used to improve:

- The flow of an incident from detection to resolution
- The experience of a change moving through assessment and approval
- The clarity and usability of a knowledge article
- The handover between teams during escalations
- The reliability of recurring operational tasks

The Maintain/Run phase was created within Humanising IT™ because **human-centred design ends at delivery**, but IT's responsibility does not.

The following section explores the significance of this additional phase, why it matters, and how it marks the point where traditional HCD stops and the strengths of ITSM take over.

Why Maintain/Run Is the Missing Half of Every Design Conversation in IT

In most organisations, design and delivery have always been treated as the finish line.

Once a service launches, the project winds down, documents are archived, and attention shifts to the next initiative.

IT carries responsibility for the service long after delivery.

Once a concept enters the real world, IT must support it, stabilise it, secure it, monitor it, respond when it fails, and carry the weight of every expectation that grows around it. IT also absorbs:

- The political pressure when outages occur
- The user frustration when friction appears
- The scrutiny of governance
- The operational responsibility of keeping something running in environments that never sit still
- The organisational turbulence of restructures, budget cuts, and shifting priorities
- The constant adaptation required as vendors, platforms, and architectures evolve beneath the service

This is the beating heart of ITSM.

Why Traditional HCD Could Never Carry the Weight of ITSM

Human-centred design grew up in environments where delivery is the natural end of the work. These are the contexts where human-centred design works exactly as intended:

- **Retail** — designing an in-store experience, checkout flow, or loyalty journey.
- **Consumer product design** — designing a wearable, appliance, or device interface.
- **Commercial services** — designing a hotel check-in flow, banking experience, or customer onboarding journey.

In these industries, once a product ships or a service launches, the design team hands over and moves on. Their work ends at delivery because they are not responsible for operating the service day-to-day.

IT is.

And the operational reality IT carries looks nothing like the environments human-centred design was built for. IT must manage:

- 24/7 availability
- Multi-vendor ecosystems
- SLAs and OLAs
- Legacy infrastructure
- Compliance and audit regimes
- Cybersecurity threats
- National critical-infrastructure obligations
- Skills shortages
- Decades of accumulated technical debt

Designing a service is a creative and analytical exercise.

Running a service in IT is an ongoing discipline of engineering, governance, risk management, coordination, and resilience.

This is the gap the HIT DDF ™ closes, extending human-centred design into the operational realities where IT services must actually survive, and ensuring that the principles and techniques of human-centred design remain present and usable in Maintain/Run.

Why this Chapter Matters

The beginning of this book explored understanding, insight, design and delivery — the work that shapes what a service *could* be.

But none of it holds if IT cannot run and maintain what it designs.

Traditional human-centred design ends where experience begins.
IT does not have that luxury.

The HIT DDF ™ goes further — not by adding more diamonds, but by anchoring design in the operational gravity that only IT carries.

Maintain/Run is the layer that protects the experience the earlier phases created.

It is where design meets reality.
It is where users form their long-term perception of IT.
It is where trust is earned, maintained, or lost.
It is where transformation becomes sustainable rather than theoretical.
And it is the moment where Humanising IT™ stops being a design philosophy and becomes a way of operating.

Applying the HIT Double Diamond Framework™ in Practice

Example: Redesigning Incident Management

To wrap up, and to understand how the HIT DDF™ works in action, the following example illustrates its application in practice.

This example walks through the redesign of an Incident Management. The purpose is not to present a "best practice" solution, but to show how understanding is built before decisions are made, and how experience is treated as part of the operating logic of IT service management.

The RIPP Trigger

The work begins with a familiar concern raised by IT leadership:

"Users are not raising tickets and are bypassing incident management processes."

At face value, this appears to be a compliance or behaviour problem. However, in Humanising IT™, this statement is treated as a **RIPP Trigger***, not as the problem itself.*

The purpose of Diamond One is to understand **what is really happening** *before deciding what to fix.*

DISCOVER

Understanding what is really happening before deciding what to do

1. RIPP

How is the problem being perceived across the organisation?

The team deliberately captures how the situation is perceived by different stakeholders:

- **Service Desk**
  "Users don't log tickets properly or at all. They email, call, or walk over instead."

- **Operations Teams**
  "We only hear about issues once they've already escalated or caused disruption."

- **Business Users**
  "Logging a ticket takes too long and doesn't help us get work done."

- **Managers**
  "We have no visibility of incidents until something goes wrong."

- **IT Leadership**
  "The process exists, but it's not being followed."

At this stage, **no attempt is made to reconcile these views.** *The goal is simply to surface how the problem is being experienced and described.*

2. Assumptions Analysis

Why does everyone see the problem this way?

Next, the assumptions underlying each perception are explored.

Examples include:

- *"If users followed the process, incidents would be handled properly."*

- *"If I log a ticket, nothing will happen quickly enough."*

- *"Escalation means the process has failed."*

- *"Control comes from enforcing compliance."*

- *"Visibility comes from tickets, not conversations."*

These assumptions explain **why stakeholders interpret the same situation differently**.

Outcome
Clarity on why different stakeholders perceive the problem in the way they do.

3. Experience Archetypes

What patterns of behaviour are emerging?

The focus now shifts from roles to **behavioural patterns**.

Across observations, several Experience Archetypes emerge, including:

- **The Workaround Expert**
  Avoids logging tickets and uses informal channels to keep work moving.

- **The Escalator**
  Bypasses the service desk to get faster attention when risk feels high.

- **The Silent Sufferer**
  Doesn't log incidents at all, absorbing friction to avoid effort or frustration.

- **The Process Guardian/Rule Enforcer/**
  Enforces ticketing rules to maintain control and reporting integrity.

- **The Blame-Shifter**

- Deflects responsibility to protect the team when outcomes are under pressure.

These archetypes describe **how people behave under current conditions**, not who they are.

4. Research: Desktop

How is the service intended to operate?

The team reviews existing artefacts, including:

- Incident management policies
- Ticket logging procedures
- Priority definitions and SLAs

- *Tool workflows and mandatory fields*
- *Reporting and compliance metrics*

This establishes the **design intent** *of the process.*

5. Research: Service Safari
How is the service actually experienced?

The team observes real work:

- *incidents raised verbally or via email*
- *tickets logged after the fact "for reporting"*
- *delays before first response*
- *users chasing updates outside the tool*
- *service desk staff reworking incomplete tickets*

These observations show how people adapt the system to get outcomes.

6. Experience Flow Sketching
How does the experience unfold over time?

Experience flows are sketched from the perspective of different archetypes.

A common flow emerges:

1. *An issue occurs*
2. *The user decides whether it's worth logging*
3. *They wait — or avoid the system*
4. *They chase progress*
5. *They escalate informally*
6. *Trust in the process decreases*

This makes friction and decision points visible.

7. Design vs Reality Review
Where does design intent break down?

The documented process assumes:
- *users will log incidents immediately*
- *information will be complete*
- *priority will be assigned correctly*
- *progress will be visible through the tool*

In reality:
- *logging feels like effort with little return*
- *progress is opaque*
- *escalation works better than compliance*
- *reporting happens after the work is done*

The gap between intent and reality becomes explicit.

8. Moments That Matter
Where is trust gained or lost?
Key moments are identified, including:
- *the effort required to log an incident*
- *time to first response*
- *silence after logging*
- *clarity of updates*
- *outcome after escalation*

These moments shape future behaviour more than the process itself.

9. HIT Insight Briefing
What do we now understand?
Insights from across Discover are synthesised into a shared view.

At this point, the organisation has **not redesigned the process**. *It has aligned on why bypassing occurs — and why it makes sense under current conditions.*

DEFINE / PLAN
Establishing clarity before design begins

10. Empathy Mapping

Evidence is organised to make lived experience explicit.

For example, mapping the Workaround Expert reveals:
- *what they say: "It's quicker this way."*
- *what they think: "Logging won't help."*
- *what they do: bypass formal channels*
- *what they feel: relief when progress resumes*

11. Proto-Personas

Proto-personas are created to stabilise understanding of who is most affected.

Examples include:
- *frontline staff accountable for outcomes under time pressure*
- *service desk analysts balancing throughput and quality*
- *managers needing early visibility of risk*

Each proto-persona may exhibit multiple archetypes.

12. Insight Synthesis

The team identifies the core insight:

The incident process optimises for reporting and control, not progress or visibility — driving bypass behaviour.

13. Problem Framing

The problem is reframed from behaviour to conditions:

"Users bypass incident management because the process does not reliably help them move work forward."

14. How Might We

Opportunity questions are opened, such as:

- How might we reduce effort at the point of logging?
- How might we make progress visible without escalation?
- How might we acknowledge informal reporting without encouraging bypass?

15. Prioritisation & Alignment Workshop

IT and the business agree where to intervene first and why.

DEVELOP / DESIGN

Exploring and shaping possible responses

16. Ideation

Ideas are generated in response to the reframed problem.

17. Low-Fidelity Prototyping

Concepts are made tangible enough to test.

18. Co-design and User Experience Testing

Concepts are explored with people who live with the process.

19. Iteration & Refinement

Options are refined based on learning.

20. Opportunity Alignment Workshop

A shared decision is made on what to take forward.

DELIVER / BUILD / TRANSITION

Proving the service will work in the real world

21–24. Validation, Build, Testing, and Release

The redesigned approach is validated, built, tested, and made ready for live operation.

MAINTAIN / RUN

Where experience proves the design

Once live, the focus is on ensuring that:

- *services continue to support people in getting work done*
- *process design does not drift away from lived reality*
- *new pressures or unintended consequences are recognised early*
- *experience remains part of day-to-day operational decision-making*

In Humanising IT™, Maintain / Run ensures that IT processes and services **remain human-centred over time**, *rather than slowly reverting to control, compliance, or convenience.*

What began as a perceived compliance issue was revealed to be a ***design problem***.

HIT DDF™ does not redesign Incident Management as a static process. It redesigns the **conditions that shape behaviour inside it** — and treats experience as part of the operational reality of ITSM.

Closing Reflection

What Changes Once You See IT This Way

By the end of this book, nothing about ITSM has been rejected. Processes still matter. Governance still matters. Stability still matters.

What has changed is *where understanding comes from*.

Throughout these chapters, you have not been asked to imagine a better future or adopt a new mindset. You have been asked to look more carefully at what is already happening, how services are designed, how people actually work, and how behaviour emerges when systems meet real conditions.

Once you see that clearly, several things become difficult to ignore.

You start to notice that many "process issues" are actually design tensions.

That repeated non-compliance is often rational adaptation.
That escalation, workarounds, silence, and heroics are signals — not failures of professionalism.
That services do not succeed or fail at handover, but in the environments they must survive.
Humanising IT™ does not add experience as a layer on top of service management.

It treats experience as evidence — something observable, interpretable, and designable.

This changes how problems are framed.
It changes when decisions are made.
It changes what data is trusted — and what is missing.

It changes how improvement work begins.

Most importantly, it changes what IT teams are accountable *for*.

Not just uptime.
Not just compliance.
Not just throughput.

But for whether a service makes sense to the people who must rely on it under pressure.

As automation and AI become more embedded in service delivery, this matters even more. Technology accelerates whatever logic already exists in the system. If that logic is misaligned with how work is actually done, automation simply scales friction faster.

If this book has done its job, you will not walk away with a checklist or a framework to apply mechanically. You will walk away with a different lens one that makes certain patterns visible, certain questions unavoidable, and certain shortcuts harder to justify.

ITSM does not need to become something else.
It needs to become more aware about the reality it is serving.

And that is Humanising IT™.

Made in the USA
Coppell, TX
17 February 2026

71702664R00105